NAVIGATING COMPLEXITY AND SYSTEM CHALLENGES:

FOUNDATIONS FOR THE A3 MODEL

ARAM AANAVAM ADHIKARAM

VENDAN ANANDA KUMARARAJAH

Printed in the United Kingdom.

Cover design and internal diagrams by Vendan Ananda Kumararajah.

For more information, visit:

www.vendan.digital

or contact: vendan@vendan.digital

Navigating Complexity and System Challenges: Foundations for the A3 Model

CONTENTS

DEDICATION

To the cherished memory of my father, Kanagaretnam Ananda Kumararajah, FCMI, FBAE ***(1937-2022)***

whose quiet strength, principled life, and unwavering pursuit of knowledge continue to guide and inspire this work.

To my mother, Sarvalogeswari, for her steadfast love and strength of spirit.

To my sisters Kanthini, Kumudini, Anandi, and Lakshmi Narayani for their enduring encouragement, presence, and belief in my purpose.

To my brother, Sabapathy, whose shared curiosity, conversations, and companionship have enriched this vision.

This work is a living continuation of my father's ideals and a tribute to the foundation my family has given me.

METHODOLOGICAL CLARIFICATION: ROLE OF AI IN EDITION DEVELOPMENT

In preparing this work, artificial intelligence (AI) tools were utilized strictly for editorial purposes, including structural refinement, linguistic clarity, and formatting consistency. At no stage were AI tools employed for the creation, conceptual development, or authorship of core content, original arguments, or theoretical frameworks.

All intellectual contributions including the formulation of the A3 Model (Aram, Aanavam, Adhikaram), its derived metrics, and its applications across multiple domains are solely the work of the author. The philosophical synthesis, conceptual mappings, and recursive grammar underpinning this edition were developed independently, without input or suggestion from AI systems.

Clear methodological boundaries governed the editorial process:

- AI was not used to propose, influence, or revise theoretical constructs, frameworks, or arguments.
- No AI-generated content was incorporated that introduced, altered, or expanded substantive conceptual material.

- Philosophical references, system mappings, and metaphysical integrations were curated manually with direct scholarly engagement.

Accordingly, the use of AI remained strictly instrumental, serving only to enhance clarity and consistency without compromising the integrity of authorship. This methodological transparency affirms the ethical commitment to epistemic stewardship, a principle foundational to the A3 Model itself. The author takes full responsibility for the final content and any errors that remain.

INTEGRITY AND ORIGINALITY STATEMENT

The A3 Model - including its foundational triadic structure of Aram (ethical coherence), Aanavam (systemic distortion), and Adhikaram (legitimate agency), together with its derived metrics and implementation pathways is the original intellectual work of the author. To the best of the author's knowledge, based on an extensive review of the literature, no prior framework in systems theory, cybernetics, or AI governance has articulated this specific architecture.

All external references (e.g., VUCA, the Rumsfeld Matrix, Critical Systems Thinking, Radical Uncertainty, environmental science) are fully cited and serve solely to contextualize the A3 Model within broader academic and professional discourses.

The originality of this work is further affirmed by transparent methodological boundaries: AI tools were employed exclusively for editorial refinement and formatting. All conceptual development, theoretical synthesis, and systemic articulation are the author's own.

AUTHOR PROFILE

Vendan Ananda Kumararajah is a strategic management professional and digital transformation expert based in the UK. He holds an MBA from the University of Derby and is a Member of the Chartered Management Institute (MCMI).

As a MIT Transformation Architect (CXO Transform) and certified practitioner in Business Transformation Management Methodology (BTM2), Kumararajah specializes in digital maturity assessment and technology innovation for organizations undergoing digital evolution. His expertise spans value creation applied behavioural science, strategy design, and systems thinking credentials that inform his approach to emerging technology governance.

Kumararajah is an active author focusing on complex systems and academic publications, with two upcoming titles in development. His work combines rigorous academic research with practical insights for policy and business leaders navigating technological transformation.

His diverse professional background in digital transformation and strategic management positions him as a thought leader on the intersection of technology, governance, and organizational change in the modern era.

He is the creator of the A3 Model, a recursive framework for ethical intelligence and adaptive legitimacy in AI governance.

HOW TO READ THIS BOOK

This book is not designed to be read in a single linear sweep, but as a layered journey. Each section serves a distinct purpose, and together they prepare you for the forthcoming *A3 Manifesto*. Depending on your background and interests, you may engage with it in different ways:

For the First-Time Reader

- Begin with the Prologue: The Recursive Age, which frames the historical and philosophical urgency of our time.
- Continue sequentially through Chapters 1–4 to gain grounding in complexity, systems, and discourses. Each chapter builds on the last and ends with Reflection Prompts to help you connect theory with your own context.

For the Practitioner or Policy Leader

- Start with the A3 Model - The Core Triad in Brief for a concise overview of Aram (ethical coherence), Aanavam (distortion awareness), and Adhikaram (agency fitness).
- Then move to the Appendices, which translate the model into implementation: the *Conceptual Primer,*

Pilot Pathway, and *Case Vignettes* show how A3 can be applied to governance, AI, and systemic transformation.

- Use these sections as a reference manual for diagnostic tools such as the *Aram Ethical Viability Test (AEVT)*, the *Aanavam Distortion Resolution Tracker (ADRT)*, and the *Agency Fitness Index (AFI)*.

3. For the Academic or Researcher

- Pay particular attention to the chapters on Systems, Discourses, and Complexity, which position A3 within wider traditions of cybernetics, systems theory, and critical thought.
- The Methodological Clarification explains how AI tools were used only for editing and not for conceptual authorship, ensuring epistemic integrity.
- The Glossary and References provide an academic anchor and situate A3 in dialogue with contemporary scholarship.

4. For the Reflective Learner

- Each chapter ends with Reflection Prompts. These are not add-ons but invitations to practice self-reflective awareness in your own context diagnosing distortions, aligning with ethical coherence, and assessing capability.
- The Epilogue: Prelude to the Manifesto reframes the entire journey as an opening, not a conclusion. It invites you to see yourself as a participant in shaping systemic intelligence.

A Note on Style

The prose moves between diagnosis and design, philosophy, and practice. Some passages are dense by necessity, engaging with ontology, ethics, and civilizational thought while others are practical and instructional. Read it iteratively, not hurriedly, returning to sections as concepts deepen.

The Reader's Role

This book is a foundation, not a finished system. It diagnoses crises and frames principles; the *A3 Manifesto* provides the executable architecture. Read with curiosity, scepticism, and openness. Treat it less as a manual, and more as a recursive companion: a text you return to as contexts shift and new systemic challenges arise.

PROLOGUE: THE RECURSIVE AGE

What This Chapter Explores: *By the end of the Prologue, you will understand why the defining feature of our era is not control but recursion, a continuous ethical process that enables systems to adapt, realign, and regenerate with integrity. You will learn how today's interlocking crises like climate change, AI disruption, institutional collapse, and social fragmentation reflect a deeper ontological breakdown in how we know, govern, and act. You'll be introduced to the A3 Model as a triadic grammar of Aram (ethical coherence), Aanavam (systemic distortion), and Adhikaram (agency fitness), and grasp how it reframes recursion as a moral compass for navigating complexity, restoring legitimacy, and cultivating systemic intelligence in an age of rapid change.*

THE RECURSIVE AGE

We have entered not just an era of rapid change, but an age defined by self-reflecting systems and pervasive feedback loops; an age of recursion. Here, transformation begins with the observer as much as the observed.

This is not another book about complexity theory or systems thinking, though it draws deeply from both. It is not another treatise on artificial intelligence or governance, though these domains permeate every page. This is a book about the fundamental crisis of meaning, legitimacy, and coherence that defines our historical moment and about the possibility of a new form of systemic intelligence capable of navigating the recursive loops of our interconnected reality.

We are living through a "polycrisis", a convergence of ecological, technological, geopolitical, and existential breakdowns that feed and amplify one another. These are not isolated problems with discrete solutions. They are entangled expressions of a deeper systemic crisis, one that demands an equally systemic response. Climate change accelerates technological desperation. Artificial intelligence transforms governance. Governance shapes technological development. Social fragmentation undermines institutional capacity. And institutional failure accelerates social fragmentation. These are not separate problems requiring distinct solutions; they are expressions of a deeper systemic crisis that demands a fundamentally innovative approach to thinking, acting, and governing.

Yet the instruments we rely on, our policies, paradigms, and institutions were forged in a world of linearity, stability, and control. They were never meant to govern recursion, emergence, or algorithmic autonomy. Our institutions were built for a world of stability and not for recursive adaptation. Our governance models presume human agency, not autonomous code. Our ethical frameworks were designed for individual action, not systemic transformation. The result is not merely ineffectiveness but a form of systemic drift, a gradual disconnection from the sources of meaning, legitimacy, and coherence that once anchored human civilization.

This book emerges from a recognition that the crisis we face is not merely technical or political but ontological, a crisis of being, knowing, and acting in a world where the foundations of existence have become fluid, interconnected, and recursively self-transforming. It is a crisis that demands not just new policies or technologies but a new form of consciousness, one capable of thinking and acting systemically, ethically, and adaptively within the recursive loops of our emerging reality.

Most people understand recursion as a technical process, especially in computing, where problems are broken down into subproblems with defined base cases. But A3 recursion is of a fundamentally different order. It is ethical, living, and non-terminating. Instead of solving static problems, it governs the alignment of dynamic systems by continually adjusting for ethical coherence (Aram), systemic distortion (Aanavam), and rightful agency (Adhikaram). This marks a shift from recursion as a computational tool to recursion as a moral and systemic compass designed to sustain integrity in the face of complexity, not just solve for it.

The framework that emerges from this inquiry - the A3 Model draws from one of humanity's oldest wisdom traditions: Tamil Saiva Siddhantam. This ancient metaphysical system offers a triadic understanding of existence through Pati (the Ground of Being), Pasu (the bound agent), and Paasam (the relational bonds that define experience). From this foundation, the A3 Model proposes a new architecture for systemic intelligence: Aram (ethical alignment), Aanavam (distortion and entropy), and Adhikaram (rightful agency).

This is not a mere academic exercise or abstract speculation. The A3 Model is designed as a practical framework for governance, transformation, and decision-making in an age where systems must be capable of continuous self-reflection, ethical alignment, and adaptive response. It offers tools for organizations grappling with digital transformation, for policymakers navigating artificial intelligence, for leaders seeking to restore legitimacy in governance, and for individuals trying to maintain coherence in an increasingly complex world.

The pages that follow trace a journey from diagnosis to design from an understanding of why our existing systems are failing to a vision of what might replace them. We explore the nature of complexity not as a problem to be solved but as a condition to be navigated with wisdom, humility, and ethical clarity. We examine systems not as mechanical assemblages but as living, adaptive, and meaning-making entities. We consider governance not as control but as stewardship, the cultivation of conditions in which systems can evolve toward greater coherence, justice, and flourishing.

The stakes of this inquiry are civilizational. We are witnessing the emergence of artificial intelligences that may soon surpass human cognitive capacity. We are experiencing ecological disruptions that threaten the foundations of human civilization. We are living through social transformations that challenge the basic assumptions of governance, identity, and community. The question is not whether we will navigate these transitions successfully, but whether we will do so with wisdom, integrity, and care for the common good.

This book is written for those who sense that we stand at a threshold not merely of technological change but of consciousness itself. It is for leaders who recognize that the challenges we face cannot be met with the same thinking that created them. It is for practitioners who seek frameworks that integrate ancient wisdom with contemporary urgency. And it is for anyone who believes that the future of human flourishing depends on our capacity to think, act, and govern recursively with awareness of the feedback loops that connect our actions to their consequences, our choices to their contexts, and our individual agency to the collective systems that shape our shared reality.

The recursive age demands self-referential intelligence. This book is an invitation to cultivate that intelligence not as an abstract intellectual exercise but as a practical necessity for navigating the challenges and opportunities of our time. The journey begins with recognition that the world we inhabit is not the world we inherited, and that the systems we need have yet to be imagined, much less created.

What follows is both a diagnosis of our current predicament and a blueprint for transformation. It is a work of philosophy grounded in practice, of ancient wisdom applied to contemporary challenges, of systemic thinking oriented toward ethical action. Most importantly, it is an invitation to participate in the creation of new forms of intelligence capable of meeting the evolving complexity of our age with wisdom, courage, and hope.

The future will be recursive. The only question is: will we shape it with conscious intent, or be unconsciously shaped by it? This book chooses the former and invites you to do the same.

This prologue serves as the gateway to a deeper exploration of complexity, systems, and the emergence of recursive intelligence as humanity's next evolutionary imperative. The journey ahead requires not just understanding but transformation of our thinking, our institutions, and ourselves.

CHAPTER-END REFLECTION PROMPTS

- Where do you experience recursive feedback loops in your life, organization, or society?

- Do you agree that current systems are unfit to govern emergence and autonomy? Why or why not?

- What does it mean to think ethically within recursion rather than outside of it?

A3 MODEL – THE CORE TRIAD IN BRIEF

At its heart, the A3 Model is a living loop that keeps systems ethical, distortion-aware, and fit to act in changing environments.

- **Aram** (Ethical Coherence) - The moral and systemic baseline. Decisions are legitimate only when they align with purpose, fairness, and sustainability.
- **Aanavam** (Distortion Awareness) - The vigilance function. Detects and localises the forces that erode coherence from bias and goal drift to feedback corruption and ethical blindness.
- **Adhikaram** (Legitimate Agency) - The capability gate. Ensures the right to act is earned and maintained through knowledge, execution capacity, governance, experience, and the ability to absorb change.

THE A3 MODEL CORE TRIAD

Recursion of Ethics, Distortion, and Agency

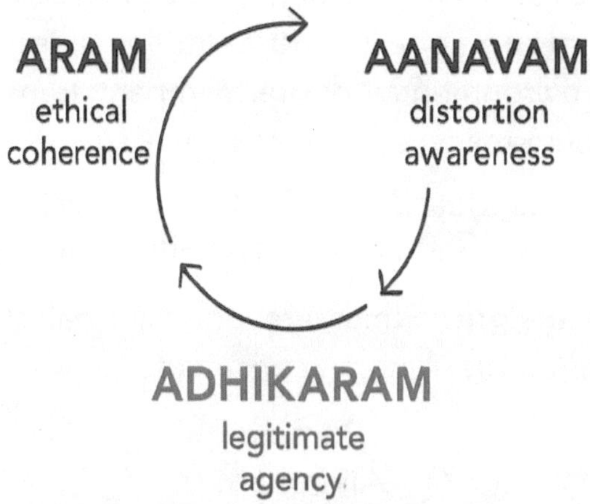

The loop runs continuously: **Aram** defines what should happen → **Aanavam** checks what is going wrong → **Adhikaram** decides whether the system is fit to proceed, pause, or withdraw.

For full operational definitions, metrics, and runtime guards, see Appendices A - D.

A3 Cybernetics at a glance - Ethics, Distortion, Agency in Recursive Governance

Purpose

The A3 Model is a neworder cybernetic framework for autonomous and hightempo environments where governance must match the speed and complexity of technology. It integrates three cotemporal pillars of Aram (ethical coherence), Aanavam (distortion awareness), and Adhikaram (legitimate agency) into a machinetempo recursive loop that decides when systems may act, must pause, or must withdraw.

Aram - Ethical Coherence

- **Role:** Set enforceable ethical conditions for action.
- **Core tests:** Purpose alignment; justice and stakeholders; proportionality and harm limits; legal/normative fit; environmental/longterm impact; transparency and accountability; ethical override paths.
- **Runtime guard:** AEVT (Aram Ethical Viability Test) blocks or suspends flows on critical ethical breaches.
- **Key insight:** Ethics are not external checklists but computable, runtime constraints.

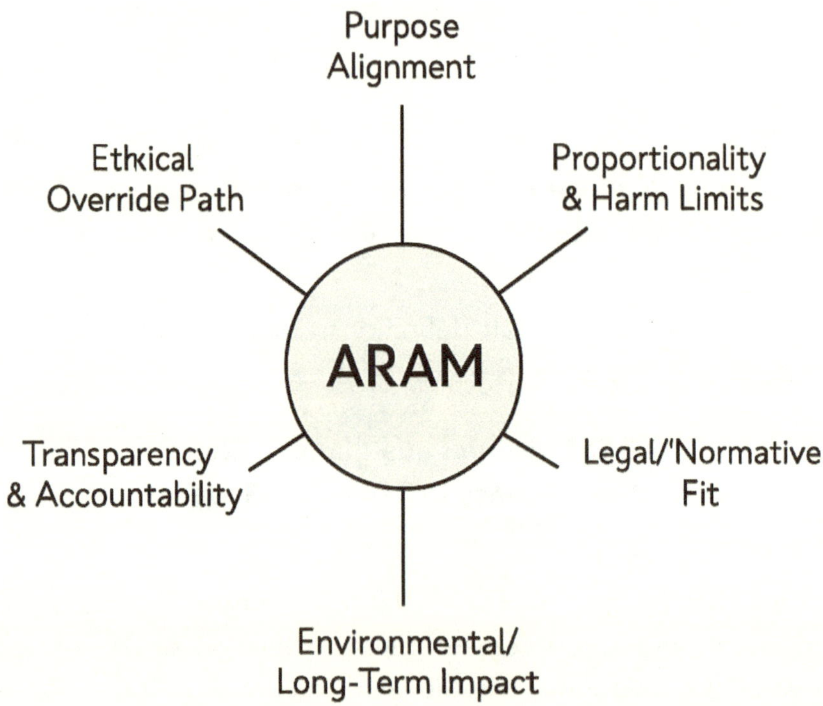

Aanavam - Distortion Awareness

- Role: Detect and classify systemic distortions that threaten coherence or legitimacy.
- Six domains: Epistemic; Structural/Organisational; Psychological/Relational; Temporal/Recursive; Environmental/Contextual; Ethical.
- Runtime guard: ADRT (Aanavam Distortion Resolution Tracker) enforces severitygraded responses from targeted guardrails to full suspension/rollback.
- Key insight: Vigilance is continuous - distortion detection is integrated into operation, not left to afterincident audit.

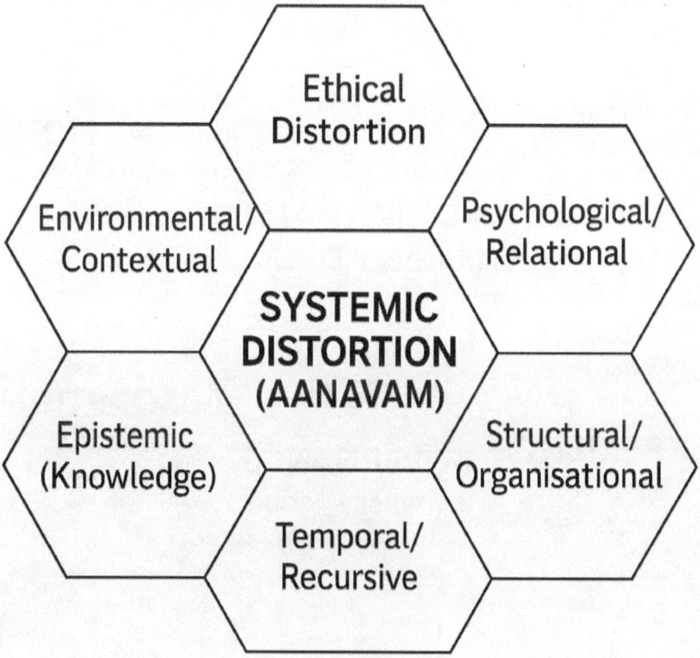

Adhikaram - Legitimate Agency

- Role: Gate the right to act based on realtime fitness.

- Five capacities: Knowledge; Action; Experience; Absorption; Governance.
- Runtime guard: AFI (Agency Fitness Index) caps autonomy tiers and can downgrade or revoke authority midrun when fitness drops.
- Key insight: Agency is earned and retained dynamically, not granted permanently.

The Recursive Loop

- Aram asks: Should this be done? Ethical thresholds decide legitimacy.

- Aanavam asks: What is distorting coherence? Distortion is localized and constrained.
- Adhikaram asks: Is the system fit to act now? Authority is gated and restored conditionally.
- Outcome: Continuous diagnosis, correction, and renewal reducing governance latency from hours/days to cycles/seconds.

Why it is different

- Neworder cybernetics: Ethics, distortion, and agency are structurally inseparable.
- Machinetempo governance: Operates at the speed of autonomous systems.
- Selfrecalibrating: Systems withdraw, learn, and reenter under rule, not discretion.
- Universal scope: Applicable to AI, organizations, infrastructure, and planetary governance.

> *"In A3, ethics is the law, distortion is the sentry, and agency is the privilege renewed in every cycle."*

AUTHOR'S NOTE

On the Path to the A3 Manifesto

This book, ***Navigating Complexity and System Challenges; Foundations for the A3 Model*** was written to confront the pressing crises of our time ranging from ecological collapse and institutional decay to the ethical ambiguities introduced by artificial intelligence and deep technological convergence. It is not merely a diagnosis, but a preparation.

This edition serves as a conceptual and philosophical prelude to the *A3 Manifesto: A New Order in Cybernetics and Systemic Intelligence*. Together, they form a dual structure: the former uncovering the fault lines of legacy paradigms, and the latter proposing a new architecture of self-referential ethical intelligence.

In these pages, I draw from civilizational knowledge, especially Tamil Saiva Siddhantam to frame the challenges of our current age as fundamentally systemic and ethical in nature. The triadic structures explored here: Pati, Pasu, and Paasam would eventually evolve into the A3 Model's architecture of Aram, Aanavam, and Adhikaram.

While this volume lays the ground by examining complexity, systems theory, transformation, and philosophy, the A3 Manifesto completes the arc. It offers a formal model of living systemic intelligence capable of navigating our interwoven crises; technical, organizational, planetary, and civilizational.

I invite readers of this book to approach it not only as a standalone exploration but as the necessary precursor to a larger systemic unfolding.

This volume builds upon conceptual foundations introduced in my earlier work, released via Amazon KDP, which explored the initial contours of recursive governance and ethical systems. Navigating Complexity and System Challenges: Leadership for the 21st century Kindle Edition by Vendan Ananda Kumararajah.

Vendan Ananda Kumararajah

Author of the A3 Model

CHAPTER 1:
INTRODUCTION

What this Chapter explores: *In this chapter, you will explore the converging macro-environmental and technological ruptures that define our era; from ecological collapse and climate acceleration to AI disruption, social destabilization, and the erosion of institutional legitimacy. You will gain insight into how these crises are not isolated incidents but interlinked expressions of deeper systemic incoherence. The chapter introduces Tamil Saiva Siddhantam not merely as a historical or metaphysical doctrine, but as a living systems grammar, one that provides ethical, epistemological, and ontological tools for understanding and navigating complexity. By integrating ancient insights with contemporary systems thinking, this chapter lays the groundwork for the A3 Model as a new-order response to our recursive age.*

1.1 Background

As we advance into the second quarter of the 21st century, there is visible instability in the global macro environment. This is not limited to technological shifts, which present both unprecedented opportunities and existentially severe risks. Governance and policymaking now face their most challenging landscape yet, one marked by rapid change, complex interdependencies, and diminishing confidence in conventional strategic responses.

We are constantly faced with uncertainty, but to varying levels and depths. Recent shifts signify a distinct inflection point that demands a fundamental reassessment of paradigms across personal, institutional, and global levels. The stability of yesterday no longer assures resilience for tomorrow.

For centuries, scientific rigour has provided the foundation for understanding and shaping institutions, economies, and societies. Yet, today's technological convergence of artificial intelligence, autonomous systems, and deep tech innovations has shattered longstanding assumptions about control, governance, and decision-making. We are no longer engaging with tools; we are negotiating with non-human intelligences whose agency disrupts human-centric governance models This profound disruption, characterized by self-amplifying feedback loops and emergent behaviours, demands that we go beyond reactive or speculative strategies.

We must seek integrative wisdom that can illuminate our way forward. In this context, ancient philosophies and civilisational worldviews may offer more than just moral or spiritual insight. They may provide practical guidance on navigating systemic challenges.

If today's governance models struggle to reconcile autonomy, emergence, and ethical coherence, ancient wisdom may offer systemic clarity. Tamil Saiva Siddhantam, through its triadic model of Pati (the Whole), Pasu (the individual entity), and Paasam (the relational bonds) does not merely provide philosophical depth but a **functional architecture for navigating complexity**.

Its relevance lies in its systemic framing of existence, offering a timeless lens through which to understand our interconnected world.

Today's accelerating complexity is not a mere escalation in scale or speed; it signals a profound rupture in **foundational epistemologies**. Governance, ethics, and decision-making were historically designed for a world of **linearity, predictability, and control**, a world that no longer exists.

In an environment shaped by emergence, autonomy, and planetary entanglement, the failure to embed living, ethical recursion within systems is no longer merely a philosophical concern; it is a civilizational existential risk.

This book proposes that without continuous systemic ethical renewal, no system: technical, organizational, societal can remain viable across evolving complexity.

The A3 Model does not seek incremental refinements to governance frameworks, it introduces a **fundamentally new systemic paradigm**, designed for an age where autonomy, recursion, and ethical alignment are not optional but **prerequisites for survival**.

The key focus in this book is a natural systemic triad that outlines how individuals and institutions perform, engage, align, and transform within broader entities. The consilience of ancient frameworks like Pati-Pasu-Paasam with contemporary challenges like artificial intelligence, governance, complexity, and transformation is what drives the development of the A3 model: Aram (ethical coherence), Aanavam (distortion awareness), and Adhikaram (legitimate agency). The ancient approach to human agency, consciousness, harmony with environment serve as a foundation to negotiating with an unpredictable and constantly evolving dynamic.

1.2 Some Destabilising Factors

1.2.1. Climate Change and Global Warming

- **Rising Temperatures:**
- The accumulation of greenhouse gases such as carbon dioxide, methane, and nitrous oxide from fossil fuel combustion, deforestation, and industrial processes is driving a measurable increase in Earth's average temperature. This warming trend is linked to altered weather patterns, more frequent heatwaves, and prolonged droughts.
- **Extreme Weather Events:**
- Climate change is intensifying storms, hurricanes, and heavy rainfall events. These extremes cause widespread damage, disrupt infrastructure, and stress disaster response systems, contributing to heightened economic and human costs.
- **Sea Level Rise:**
- As global temperatures rise, polar ice caps and glaciers melt, causing rising sea levels. Coastal cities are particularly vulnerable, facing increased flood risks, saltwater intrusion into freshwater supplies, and eventual population displacement.

1.2.2 Resource Depletion and Unsustainable Consumption

- **Finite Natural Resources:**
- Traditional resources such as fossil fuels, freshwater, and mineral deposits are being extracted at rates far exceeding natural replenishment. This overconsumption threatens long-term resource security and drives geopolitical tensions over access.
- **Overexploitation of Renewable Resources:**
- Even renewable resources such as forests and fisheries are under stress when extraction exceeds sustainable limits. Overfishing, deforestation, and unsustainable agricultural practices lead to land degradation and biodiversity loss.
- **Economic Pressures and Wasteful Consumption:**
- The prevailing global economic model often prioritises short-term gains, encouraging mass production and consumption without adequate recycling or reuse. This linear model not only depletes resources but also creates mounting waste-management challenges.

This pattern of overconsumption and reckless conduct reveals a deep-seated *Aanavam*, a distortion where short-term economic pressures override the *Aram* required for long-term stewardship.

- **1.2.3 Biodiversity Loss and Ecosystem Degradation**
- **Habitat Destruction:**
- Urbanisation, industrial expansion, and infrastructure development fragment natural ecosystems, leading to habitat loss. The clearing of forests and wetlands disrupts the intricate balance of species that these environments support.

- **Species Extinction:**
- Rapid changes in land use, climate shifts, and pollution are driving many species toward extinction. Biodiversity loss undermines ecosystem resilience, diminishing nature's ability to provide essential services such as pollination, water purification, and carbon sequestration.
- **Disruption of Ecological Networks:**
- The removal or decline of key species can have cascading effects throughout ecosystems. Such disruptions may lead to uncontrolled pest outbreaks, invasive species dominance, and a subsequent decline in ecosystem services crucial to human well being.

The rapid decline in biodiversity is a critical symptom of *Aanavam*, reflecting a systemic failure to embed the *Aram* of ecological value into our models of development.

1.2.4 Pollution and Environmental Degradation

- **Air Pollution:**
- Emissions from vehicles, industrial facilities, and power plants contribute significantly to poor air quality. Airborne pollutants (particulates, nitrogen oxides, sulphur dioxide) not only harm human health, causing respiratory and cardiovascular diseases, but also impact plant and animal life.
- **Water Contamination:**
- Industrial discharges, agricultural runoff, and improper waste disposal introduce toxic substances into water bodies. This pollution compromises drinking water supplies, harms aquatic ecosystems, and disrupts food chains.

- **Soil Degradation:**
- Overuse of chemical fertilisers and pesticides, along with improper disposal of industrial waste, deteriorates soil quality. This degradation affects agricultural productivity and creates long-term challenges for sustaining food security.
- **Plastic and Chemical Waste:**
- The proliferation of single-use plastics and persistent chemicals has led to widespread contamination. Microplastics in aquatic systems and soils are emerging as significant concerns, with potential long-term impacts on health and biodiversity.

Widespread environmental contamination acts as a clear indicator of *Aanavam*, where the externalized costs of industrial activity highlight a profound disconnect from the *Aram* of public and ecological health. Resulting Adhikaram (Agency) is flawed governance.

1.2.5 Social Equity and Environmental Justice

- **Unequal Impacts:**
- Environmental degradation and climate change do not affect all communities equally. Marginalised and low-income populations often face higher exposure to pollutants, fewer resources to adapt, and less political influence to safeguard their interests.
- **Access to Clean Resources:**
- Issues such as water scarcity and air pollution disproportionately impact vulnerable groups. Ensuring equitable access to clean water, clean air, and a healthy environment is a fundamental component of social equity.

- **Community Resilience:**
- Building sustainable communities requires integrating social justice into environmental planning. This entails involving local stakeholders in decision-making, improving infrastructure in underserved areas, and ensuring a fair distribution of environmental benefits and burdens.

These inequities expose a fundamental *Aanavam* within our governance systems, demonstrating a failure of *Aram* to ensure that the burdens of environmental degradation do not fall disproportionately on the most vulnerable. Therefore, capacity building (Adhikaram) is distorted or inconsistent.

1.2.6 Economic and Industrial Transformations

- **Transition to Renewable Energy:**
- The urgent need to reduce carbon emissions is driving a global shift from fossil fuels to renewable energy sources such as wind, solar, and hydroelectric power. This transition addresses climate change while creating opportunities for sustainable economic growth.
- **Circular Economy Models:**
- The traditional linear economy of "take, make, dispose" is gradually being replaced by circular economy principles. Emphasis is placed on maximising resource use, promoting recycling and reuse, and reducing waste, thereby alleviating pressure on natural resources.

Technological advances, when aligned with governance frameworks such as A3, can embed sustainability metrics into industrial processes, ensuring innovation supports ecological stewardship rather than accelerating resource depletion. The push toward circular models can be seen as an attempt to exercise *Adhikaram*, the legitimate agency to correct the *Aanavam* of the linear economy and realign with a more sustainable *Aram*.

1.2.7 Innovative Technologies and Sustainability

Advances in digital technology, automation, and data analytics are increasingly being harnessed to enhance resource efficiency and reduce environmental impact across industries. Emerging tools such as precision agriculture, smart manufacturing, and realtime energy monitoring systems enable organisations to track and optimise their use of water, energy, and raw materials.

Artificial intelligence and machine learning models can forecast demand, detect inefficiencies, and recommend interventions that reduce waste and emissions. In engineering domains, the integration of environmental performance metrics into control systems, such as those informed by the A3 model, allows for real-time adaptive monitoring, diagnosis, and adjustment of industrial processes in line with sustainability objectives.

For example, coupling computational fluid dynamics (CFD) with A3governed decision rules can optimise heating, cooling, and ventilation systems in manufacturing plants, significantly lowering energy consumption while maintaining operational quality. Similar approaches in logistics where route optimisation algorithms are guided by both cost and carbon-intensity metrics demonstrate how technical innovation can be steered toward broader environmental goals.

Importantly, technology alone does not guarantee sustainability; its deployment must be embedded within governance frameworks that ensure ethical coherence (*Aram*), actively identify and correct systemic distortions (*Aanavam*), and validate the fitness of action (*Adhikaram*). In this sense, the A3 model serves not only as a diagnostic tool but also as an operational compass, ensuring that industrial innovation advances environmental stewardship rather than accelerating resource depletion.

1.2.8 From Isolated Crises to Systemic Realignment

The global challenges we face in the realms of environment and sustainability are vast and interconnected. Addressing them requires a holistic approach that goes beyond technological fixes. It involves:

- Integrating ethical and equitable frameworks into design and policy.
- Rethinking economic models toward sustainability and circularity.
- Promoting resilient communities and ecosystems that can adapt to changing conditions.

Taken together, these destabilising factors represent not merely discrete environmental challenges, but interconnected expressions of systemic imbalance. Within the A3 framework, they can be read as domains where *Aanavam* or systemic distortion emerges through unsustainable practices, inequitable governance, and fragmented responses.

Addressing them requires not only technical solutions but the recursive interplay of *Aram* (ethical coherence), *Aanavam* diagnosis, and *Adhikaram* (legitimate capability to act) to realign systems toward long-term viability.

In this view, climate, resource, biodiversity, pollution, equity, and economic transitions are not isolated policy arenas, but components of a single adaptive system whose stability depends on ethically grounded, capability-driven governance.

1.3 Deep Tech Integration

Artificial intelligence leads the current wave of technological disruption. IoT, quantum computing, blockchain, nanotechnology, and augmented reality are rapidly transforming how we live, work, and govern. AI systems are already influencing agriculture, manufacturing, scientific research, and even creative domains. The scale and speed of impact are overwhelming.

As technology advances beyond human cognition and agency, governance faces an existential dilemma. Hyperautomation, where machines assume once-human decisions raises urgent ethical concerns about **control, sovereignty, and systemic integrity**.

This is compounded by the considerable influence of corporate and political interests that often direct these technologies, creating a deterministic trajectory with little recourse.

It is no longer just about privacy or cybersecurity. The greater risks lie in technological determinism and behavioural interventions that can shape thoughts, preferences, and behaviours at scale. Governance must evolve beyond compliance, it must embody **absorptive ethics**, structural transparency, and sovereignty that resists technological determinism.

As technology evolves to mirror human cognition and autonomy, policymakers face the immense task of crafting a harmonious partnership between humans and machines. This challenge demands that we define distinct yet complementary roles to ensure that both can contribute to society in meaningful ways.

Emerging trends in this landscape point toward hyperautomation, where technology increasingly takes over roles traditionally reserved for human decision-making. Even when initiated with the best intentions, sidelining human judgment can introduce complex risks and unintended consequences.

Moreover, there is a very real danger that profit-driven or politically motivated corporations might appropriate governance and policymaking processes. This creates a structural and strategic permanence with little recourse to correction without major political intervention, whose institutions might themselves have been compromised.

While issues like privacy, cybersecurity, and data protection are critical, they represent only part of the challenge. Leaders must also address the broader implications of enforced technological determinism and behavioural science interventions. These phenomena can subtly reshape societal norms, cultural values, and individual freedoms, often in ways that are difficult to detect until their effects are deeply entrenched. For example, AI-driven recommendation algorithms can influence consumer behaviour, political opinions, and even mental health, creating feedback loops that reinforce specific outcomes over others.

In brief, such control can lead to several systemic challenges:

- **Erosion of Human Agency**: When machines assume decision-making roles, humans risk losing their capacity to shape outcomes, diminishing their role in critical processes.
- **Technological Determinism**: An over-reliance on technology can create a deterministic mindset, where systems dictate societal norms and behaviours, often at the expense of human values.
- **Behavioural Science Interventions**: Technologies can artificially alter behavioural patterns and socio-cultural outlooks, manipulating individuals and communities in ways that may not align with their interests.

To mitigate these risks, governance and policymaking must prioritize a core set of principles: ethics, bias mitigation, transparency, and individual sovereignty and security. These principles, which align with the A3 model's emphasis on ethical purpose (Aram) and relational awareness (Aanavam), ensure that technological advancements serve humanity rather than undermine it.

Ethical governance requires:

- **Ethics:** Embedding moral considerations into technology design and deployment, ensuring alignment with societal values.
- **Bias Mitigation**: Actively addressing biases in algorithms and systems to prevent discriminatory outcomes.
- **Transparency**: Providing clear visibility into how technologies operate and make decisions, fostering trust and accountability.
- **Individual Sovereignty and Security**: Protecting individuals' rights to autonomy, privacy, and safety in an increasingly automated world.

By grounding deep tech integration in these principles, leaders can navigate the complexities of hyperautomation while safeguarding the human-machine relationship. The rise of deep tech, therefore, presents a fundamental challenge: to exercise the *Adhikaram* necessary to embed *Aram* into our technological architecture, thereby mitigating the profound *Aanavam* of unchecked automation and deterministic control.

1.3.1 Geopolitics and Global Powerplay

The global geopolitical order is undergoing reconfiguration. The unipolar dominance of the post-Cold War United States is waning. New regional powers like China, India, Russia, and Turkey are asserting influence economically, technologically, and militarily. Multilateralism is increasingly defined by tension and uncertainty.

Wars, economic sanctions, and shifting alliances have not only created instability but also precipitated mass migrations and humanitarian crises. Military interventions, such as those in Iraq, Syria, and Afghanistan, have shown that power projection without systemic foresight often results in long-term chaos.

Global institutions are struggling to mediate this complexity. A return to simplistic geopolitical narratives is no longer tenable. Understanding emergent power dynamics through a systemic lens is critical.

If we consider globalisation as irreversible, the implications for a new configuration in identity (individual, ethnic and transnational), interconnected politics, economic projections beyond traditional boundaries, influence and power, conflict management and overall institutional trajectory of States is profound. The way they manage and navigate the new dynamics will create innovative structures and governance frameworks.

We may indeed be at the biggest inflection point since World War II, facing challenges on a scale comparable to the post-war reconstruction, but now with the added complexity of global digital interconnectedness and non-state actors.

This global reconfiguration is a manifestation of systemic *Aanavam*, where the breakdown of old orders demands new forms of *Adhikaram* grounded in a more distributed and coherent global *Aram*.

1.3.2 Internal Power Dynamics

Technology has changed the structure and flow of influence within societies. The internet and social media have not only redefined communication but have also reconfigured power and engagement. The critical question is whether this creates a genuine decentralized power structure or follows a deterministic trajectory controlled by larger powers.

Marketing, public relations, learning, and even political discourse are shaped by data patterns and behavioural targeting. This redefines how organisations, states, and individuals communicate and engage. Traditional institutions such as governments, universities, and the media are challenged to adapt to these new realities or risk obsolescence.

Beyond the immediate commercial consequences of a negative social media review, online campaigns and narrative shaping can prevent a non-judgmental approach to problems or issue resolution. Very often, decisions and actions can be pressured without due course to procedure or considered thought.

The future requires a reconciliation of evolving power dynamics with the broader macro environment. Institutions must now rethink their structures and cultural norms to remain relevant. Engaging with individuals and the State, while keeping an eye on the new power dynamics will require skill and craft.

The reconfiguration of influence by digital platforms reveals a critical *Aanavam*, a distortion where authentic discourse is replaced by algorithmic determinism, challenging the very foundation of legitimate individual and institutional *Adhikaram*.

1.3.3 Migration and Demographic Changes

Mass migration, whether driven by economic, environmental, or geopolitical factors, is a defining feature of the contemporary world. Developed countries with ageing populations rely on migrant labour, while conflicts and climate change drive displacement globally.

This creates both opportunity and tension. Migration alters the cultural, economic, and institutional fabric of societies. Integration, social cohesion, and identity become areas of contestation. Nations face mounting dilemmas: how to integrate diverse populations, reconcile cultural identities, and ensure fair distribution of opportunity and responsibility. National policies must balance humanitarian obligations with systemic resilience.

With migration, identities become more fluid and complex. Transnational identities, those transcending traditional ethnic or state-defined boundaries, often shaped by cross-cultural experiences and digital connections will create new dynamics. The traditional structure and role of enshrined institutions will therefore not just be challenged but forced to evolve.

At the same time, demographic shifts are reshaping the future of work, governance, and education. Younger populations in the global south will define the labour force of the future. Aligning education, values, and capability across diverse cultures becomes paramount.

Ethical governance in this context must go beyond border control. It must recognise the ontological and systemic impacts of displacement, belonging, and identity. These shifts are not merely logistical or infrastructural, they alter the very narratives through which societies define themselves.

The demographic shifts are expressions of a deep *Aanavam* in the global system; addressing them requires an *Aram*-based approach to policy that affirms human dignity and builds the *Adhikaram* for inclusive, resilient societies.

1.4 Impact on Organisations

Organisations, institutions, and individuals are not immune to macroenvironmental shifts. In fact, they are microcosms of the broader systemic transitions. The organisational transformations and workplace shifts unfold within the same volatile environment shaped by climate change, resource pressures, social inequity, and technological disruption. These are not separate challenges but interacting forces within a single adaptive system. We will look at how the macroenvironment impacts Organisations first.

1.4.1 Transformation as a Systemic Imperative

In a volatile, interconnected world, transformation is not an occasional initiative but a continuous systemic process. Organizations exist within shifting economic, technological, environmental, and social landscapes; stability depends on their ability to adapt with coherence and purpose to the evolving realities.

In A3 terms, successful transformation demands *Aram* (ethical coherence in decision-making), *Aanavam* diagnosis (identifying systemic distortions that obstruct adaptation), and *Adhikaram* (the legitimate capability to act). In this context, transformation is not merely change, but the deliberate application of *Adhikaram* to diagnose and correct organizational *Aanavam*, guided by the constant renewal of its systemic *Aram*.

Digital and Structural Adaptation

Technological change is a primary driver of transformation. Digital transformation extends beyond deploying AI, cloud computing, automation, or data-driven strategies; it involves reshaping culture, processes, and behaviours so that technology supports long-term viability. Without structural adaptation, organizations lose relevance as markets and stakeholder expectations shift.

Example: Traditional retail chains moving to e-commerce platforms like Shopify demonstrate that technology adoption must be integrated with operational and cultural shifts to remain competitive.

Innovation as a Recurring Capability

Innovation in products, services, or operational models is essential to systemic resilience. It is not simply about novelty but about creating pathways that align with evolving user needs, technological trends, and sustainability imperatives. Organizations that fail to refresh their value proposition risk stagnation. Innovation also establishes new trajectories that enable transcending technological and business constraints and challenges.

Example: Apple's evolution from a personal computer manufacturer to a multi-device, ecosystem-based enterprise illustrates innovation as a continual cycle, not a one-off achievement.

Integration Across System Boundaries

Transformation succeeds when strategy, leadership, technology, and culture operate as an integrated system. This means recognising that change affects and is affected by all organisational subsystems. Leaders must ensure coherence between departments, processes, and external stakeholder engagement to maintain direction during change.

Example: Microsoft's shift from a software-centric model to a cloud-first, AI-powered enterprise required synchronising technical reinvention with cultural renewal.

Failure Modes in Transformation Systems

Transformation initiatives often fail when vision and execution are misaligned. Poorly articulated strategy, leadership gaps, or siloed execution can derail adaptation even when resources are available. Common risks include employee resistance, financial instability, and security vulnerabilities. Very often, leadership deficiencies cause failure more than operational efficiency because without vision and strategy, execution becomes aimless.

Example: Blockbuster's inability to adapt to the digital streaming model illustrates how ignoring systemic change signals can lead to rapid decline.

In Summary: Transformation is a dynamic process of anticipating change, aligning innovation with systemic viability, and sustaining coherence across the organisation. Within the A3 framework, this means continuously diagnosing distortions, reaffirming ethical purpose, and exercising legitimate capability to act.

1.4.2 Evolving Workplace Systems

Globalisation, technological acceleration, and shifting social expectations have transformed the workplace into a dynamic socio-technical system. The interplay of distributed teams, AI-driven processes, and new cultural norms demands that organisations actively design for adaptability and resilience.

Distributed and Remote Collaboration

Advances in connectivity have made remote and hybrid work models mainstream, enabling teams to operate across continents. While this increases access to global talent, it introduces challenges in culture, language, and social norms. Effective governance requires clear communication protocols, shared digital platforms, and inclusive practices. This offers both a challenge and opportunity.

Example: Google's globally distributed teams use structured collaboration tools and culturally sensitive practices to maintain cohesion and innovation.

Shifting Team Dynamics and Workflows

Virtual collaboration tools like Zoom, Slack, and Microsoft Teams have replaced many traditional in-office interactions. Maintaining creativity and trust in this environment requires intentional engagement strategies, such as virtual icebreakers, digital whiteboards, and structured brainstorming sessions. Reviews, assessments, and interactions work under new dynamics. Adapting to the evolving reality augments success possibility.

Example: Organisations facilitating digital design sprints replicate the collaborative energy of physical workshops, preserving creative momentum in remote settings.

The Role of AI and Hyperautomation

AI is reshaping work by automating routine tasks, providing predictive insights, and supporting decision-making. This shift requires workforce reskilling and redefinition of roles to emphasise human-machine collaboration rather than competition. Appreciating the role and capability of AI agents and their relationship to human co-workers is key.

Example: Banks using AI chatbots for customer service free human staff to oversee complex financial interactions, improving both efficiency and client experience.

Leadership and Workforce Resilience

Navigating technological and cultural change requires leaders who can foster adaptability, agility, continuous learning, and systemic awareness. Coherence in strategy and vision enhances success factors and work force efficiency. This means embedding resilience into organisational culture, so employees can respond positively to disruption.

Example: Companies with strong learning and development strategies build long-term capacity to adapt, as seen in organisations that integrate ongoing AI literacy into workforce training.

Governing this new workplace system requires leaders to actively diagnose sources of *Aanavam*, like digital friction or cultural exclusion and apply an *Aram*-centric approach to foster a resilient and capable workforce (*Adhikaram*).

In Summary

The workplace is now a living system shaped by distributed collaboration, technological augmentation, and evolving cultural expectations. In A3 terms, maintaining *Aram* ensures ethical and inclusive workplace practices; diagnosing *Aanavam* surfaces distortions such as inequity or misalignment; and cultivating *Adhikaram* builds collective capability to thrive in a changing environment.

The A3 framework provides a unifying lens, enabling leaders to interpret these pressures as manifestations of *Aanavam*, and to respond with *Aram* and *Adhikaram*. In this way, workplace transformation becomes a deliberate, governance-driven process that strengthens systemic resilience in an uncertain world.

The pace of change is unprecedented, driven by remote work, automation, and AI integration. Organisations that embrace change and foster resilient teams will thrive in this new digital era. Modern organisations operate within dynamic stakeholder ecosystems where legal requirements, regulatory constraints, ethical norms, and consumer expectations intersect.

Aligning with these diverse forces demands more than mere compliance; it requires dialogue, flexibility, and a systemic vision. Issues such as data privacy, intellectual property, and social responsibility are now strategic imperatives, not peripheral concerns.

As the macroenvironment evolves with increasing volatility, organisations serve as bridges linking individuals to wider societal and global dynamics. Their ability to adapt and maintain ethical coherence can support broader stability or, if neglected, contribute to systemic risk.

At the same time, a narrow focus on corporate outcomes may obscure deeper, long-term challenges. Technology platforms, if deployed with rigid and predeterministic logic, can constrain dialogue and outcomes to the benefit of short-term interests, but at the cost of accumulating risk and future instability. This is a recipe for short-term thrill, but long-term chaos.

1.4.3 Individual Fitness and Capability

Individual fitness and capability today is a **complex relationship between hard skills, soft skills, ontology, and ethics**. These elements shape personal and professional fitness. The key underlying areas that the A3 model covers include:

Hard Skills – The Technical Foundation

Hard skills form the measurable, technical foundation necessary for navigating complex professional and societal challenges. These skills are objective, teachable, and testable, enabling individuals to perform specific tasks with precision and expertise.

Technical proficiency encompasses mastery of tools, software, or machinery relevant to a field, such as coding in Python for a data scientist or operating advanced manufacturing equipment. Analytical reasoning involves breaking down complex problems into manageable components, using data-driven approaches to identify patterns and solutions, like a financial analyst forecasting market trends.

Domain expertise reflects deep knowledge in a specific area, such as a civil engineer's understanding of structural design or a biologist's expertise in genetic sequencing. Digital literacy is critical in an increasingly technology-driven world, enabling individuals to navigate digital platforms, interpret data visualizations, or secure systems against cyber threats.

Systems mapping allows individuals to visualize and understand interconnections within complex systems, such as mapping supply chain logistics to optimize efficiency. While these skills are essential for technical competence, they alone are insufficient without the human qualities and contextual awareness provided by soft skills, ontology, and ethics.

For example, a software engineer may excel at coding but struggle to innovate in a team without people skills or ethical considerations.

Soft Skills - The Social & Cognitive Edge

Soft skills are the interpersonal and intrapersonal competencies that define how individuals interact, adapt, and thrive in dynamic, collaborative environments. These skills enable effective engagement with others and foster resilience in rapidly changing contexts.

Communication involves articulating ideas clearly and listening actively, ensuring alignment in diverse teams such as a project manager conveying goals across departments. Empathy allows individuals to understand and value others' perspectives, fostering trust and reducing misunderstandings, as seen when a healthcare provider connects with patients to improve care outcomes.

Conflict resolution equips individuals to navigate disagreements constructively, like a mediator facilitating dialogue between stakeholders with competing interests. Collaboration drives collective success by leveraging diverse skill sets, such as cross-functional teams developing innovative products.

Leadership inspires and guides others toward shared goals, requiring vision and adaptability, as demonstrated by community leaders organizing disaster relief efforts. Learning agility reflects the ability to rapidly acquire and apply new knowledge in unfamiliar situations, such as an entrepreneur pivoting strategies during market disruptions.

These skills create coherence in multicultural and dynamic systems, enabling individuals to build strong relationships and adapt to evolving challenges and apply critical thinking.

Ontology - The State of Being

Ontology, in the A3 model, refers to an individual's relationship with themselves, their knowledge, and their perception of reality, shaping how they navigate the world. It emphasizes self-awareness and contextual understanding as critical components of decision-making and meaning-making.

Recognizing multiple ***perspectives*** allows individuals to appreciate diverse viewpoints, such as a policy analyst considering both economic and social impacts of a regulation. Understanding one's role in a system involves recognizing how personal actions influence broader networks, like a teacher shaping a classroom's learning environment.

Reflecting on ***internal distortions*** requires examining biases or assumptions that cloud judgment, such as a manager questioning their tendency to favour certain team members. Continuously realigning purpose and values ensures actions remain consistent with personal and organizational goals, as seen when a social entrepreneur adapts their mission to address emerging community needs.

Ontology fosters a deeper awareness of how individuals fit within ***complex systems***, enabling them to make decisions that are both purposeful and grounded. For example, a community organizer reflecting on their values might shift strategies to better align with local cultural contexts, enhancing their impact.

Ethics - The Guiding Principles

Ethics, in the context of the A3 model, transcends mere adherence to rules or cultural norms, representing an inner compass rooted in *Aram*, structural coherence and relational integrity. This ethical framework guides individuals through complex dilemmas and enhances their agency within systems.

Awareness of consequences involves anticipating the short- and long-term impacts of decisions, such as a corporate leader weighing the environmental costs of a new factory. Sensitivity to relational impacts ensures actions respect the needs and dignity of others, like a negotiator balancing stakeholder interests in a trade agreement.

Navigating dilemmas under complexity requires evaluating trade-offs in ambiguous situations, such as a doctor deciding between patient autonomy and medical necessity during a resource shortage. Ethical clarity strengthens systemic legitimacy by fostering trust and accountability.

For instance, in 2015, Volkswagen's emissions scandal highlighted the consequences of ethical lapses, as the company's deliberate manipulation of emissions tests eroded public trust and incurred billions in penalties. In self-regulating governance environments, where decisions feed back into systems, ethical reflexivity ensures individuals act with integrity, aligning personal actions with collective well-being.

A Holistic Approach to Fitness & Capability

The complexity of today's interconnected world demands more than isolated competencies; it requires a harmonious integration of technical mastery, interpersonal intelligence, ontological depth, and ethical alignment.

This holistic approach ensures personal and systemic viability in dynamic, unpredictable environments. Technical mastery through hard skills provides the tools to address specific challenges, while soft skills enable collaboration and adaptability in diverse settings.

Ontological depth fosters self-awareness and contextual understanding, allowing individuals to navigate systems with clarity and purpose. Ethical alignment ensures decisions are sustainable and just, fostering trust and legitimacy. Together, these elements create coherence, enabling individuals to contribute meaningfully to complex systems, whether in workplaces, communities, or global networks.

For example, a sustainable urban planner might combine technical expertise in green infrastructure, collaborative skills to engage community stakeholders, self-reflection to align with inclusive values, and ethical decision-making to prioritize equitable access to resources.

This integrated capability is essential for addressing multifaceted challenges like climate change, social inequality, and technological disruption, ensuring both personal growth and systemic resilience.

Individual fitness in this new era is a direct reflection of the A3 model in practice: the cultivation of ethical coherence (*Aram*), the awareness to navigate systemic distortions (*Aanavam*), and the technical and moral capacity to act effectively (*Adhikaram*).

Final Thoughts

This chapter has laid the foundation for understanding the ***systemic rupture*** in traditional governance and the urgent need for a new model. The A3 Model is not an iteration, but a ***reconfiguration*** capable of engaging with today's deep complexity while anchored in a timeless ontology. True fitness, be it leadership, organizational transformation, or personal development is achieved through the fusion of skills, state of being, and ethical alignment, ensuring ***adaptability and coherence*** in a world of accelerating change.

As this volume diagnoses the failures of legacy systems and maps the contours of contemporary complexity, it also prepares the ground for a deeper transformation. This transformation is articulated fully in the companion A3 Manifesto, where the core logic introduced here - Aram, Aanavam, and Adhikaram is formalised into a self-referential architecture for viable, ethical systems. The Manifesto does not simply extend this analysis; it offers a new operational grammar for systemic design, capable of governing complexity, distortion, and agency from first principles.

CHAPTER-END REFLECTION PROMPTS

- Which destabilizing forces resonate most with your own context or sector?

- Can traditional governance models evolve fast enough to manage today's systemic shifts?

- How might ancient civilizational frameworks help design future-fit systems?

CHAPTER 2: COMPLEXITY

What this Chapter explores: *In Chapter 2, you will develop a foundational understanding of complexity by distinguishing it from related concepts such as volatility, uncertainty, and ambiguity. You will gain fluency in analytical tools like the Rumsfeld Matrix and Joanna Boehnert's 16 characteristics of complex systems, learning how to interpret systemic traits such as emergence, feedback loops, and adaptive interdependence. Crucially, this chapter connects complexity to* ***ethical adaptation****, showing that in dynamic, nonlinear environments, viability depends not only on technical responses but on recursive ethical awareness. This sets the stage for you to approach complexity not as chaos to be controlled, but as a living condition to navigate with intelligence and coherence.*

The Complexity Conundrum

In the early 1990s, the U.S. Army War College introduced the acronym VUCA - Volatility, Uncertainty, Complexity, and Ambiguity to describe the shifting post-Cold War global landscape. This terminology, later adopted by strategists and leaders across fields, captures the pervasive sense of instability, fragmentation, and unpredictability that characterizes contemporary systems. Far from being merely descriptive, VUCA has become a framework for understanding the strategic and systemic challenges we now face across economic, social, technological, and ecological domains.

Complexity, in this context, is not just about complications or scale. It signals an environment where cause and effect are not linear, where outcomes are emergent, and where systems resist reduction. It introduces the idea that traditional logic may no longer be sufficient to explain outcomes or chart paths forward. The variables are numerous, the feedback loops rapid, and the interdependencies dense. Complexity is not merely a feature of large systems; it is a signature of living, adaptive, and interrelated systems where the parts cannot be fully understood in isolation.

As we move deeper into the age of AI, climate disruption, and social transformation, the complexity conundrum demands more than technical solutions. It demands a philosophical orientation and an appreciation of paradox, humility in the face of uncertainty, and a renewed attention to ethics, experience, and systemic alignment.

2.1 Volatility

Volatility refers to the speed and turbulence of change. It is characterised by rapid, often unexpected shifts, economic shocks, technological breakthroughs, political upheavals that can disrupt the assumptions and routines of everyday systems. Volatility is not new, but what distinguishes the present era is the frequency and interconnectedness of disruptions.

For example, a small regulatory change in one nation can send ripples across global markets. A tweet from a political figure can destabilize diplomacy. A minor glitch in code can crash an entire system. In volatile environments, the rate of change exceeds the pace of learning. It is not only about what is changing, but how fast and how many other domains it touches.

To cope with volatility, we must invest in real-time sensing, scenario planning, and agile organisational structures. Volatility cannot be fully eliminated, but its impact can be mitigated through anticipation, resilience planning, and systemic awareness.

2.2 Uncertainty

Uncertainty refers to the challenge of predicting outcomes when we lack full information, face conflicting data, or deal with inherent randomness like trying to forecast a storm without complete weather data. Unlike volatility (which we can often measure, like stock market swings), uncertainty includes 'unknown unknowns' that defy easy mapping. For instance, in business, it is the sudden market shift no one saw coming.

It manifests in multiple forms:

- **Epistemological uncertainty** - when we lack knowledge about a system or phenomenon. This invites deeper learning, inquiry, and sensemaking.
- **Ontological uncertainty** - when our inner state or worldview contributes to indecision. This reflects our subjective dissonance or moral ambiguity.

- **Aleatory uncertainty** - when randomness or chance disrupts even well-structured systems.

The Rumsfeld Matrix

The Rumsfeld Matrix originates from a press briefing by former U.S. Secretary of Defense Donald Rumsfeld in 2002. He described categories of knowledge relevant to decision-making and risk analysis, highlighting the challenges of dealing with uncertainty. His framework has since been widely adopted within strategy, risk management, and complexity science.

The Rumsfeld Matrix Fig. 1

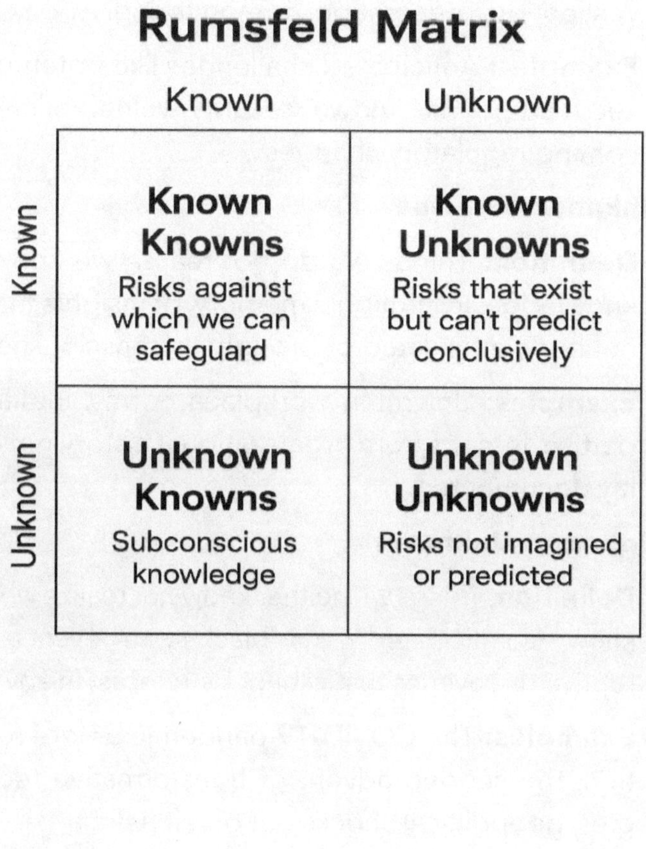

The Four Quadrants

The matrix divides knowledge into four zones:

1. Known Knowns

- **Definition:** Things we know that we know; established facts or skills that can be planned for and managed explicitly.
- **Examples:** Well-understood scientific principles, documented processes, recorded laws.

2. Known Unknowns

- **Definition:** Things we know that we do not know; identified gaps or uncertainties that require active investigation, preparation, or monitoring.
- **Examples:** Anticipated challenges like potential market disruptions, known security vulnerabilities, upcoming regulatory changes.

3. Unknown Knowns

- **Definition:** Things we do not realize we know; tacit knowledge, institutional memory, or insights that have not been articulated or brought to consciousness.
- **Examples:** Unwritten workplace norms, intuitive expertise, lessons from organizational history not explicitly documented.

4. Unknown Unknowns

- **Definition:** Things we neither know nor realize we do not know; unanticipated risks, "black swan" events, or disruptive discoveries that cannot be forecast in advance.
- **Examples:** The COVID-19 pandemic before recognition, the sudden advent of transformative technologies, geopolitical shocks out of left field.

Practical Uses

- **Risk Management:** Helps organizations map and address risks they can manage, investigate, surface, or must simply prepare to adapt to.
- **Strategic Planning:** Guides leaders to identify information gaps and recognize the limits of foresight, which encourages humility and resilience.
- **Organizational Learning:** Encourages the surfacing of tacit knowledge and the initiative-taking cultivation of adaptability for surprise events.

Key Insights

- The matrix underscores that not all uncertainty is the same: some can be planned for, while others are fundamentally unpredictable.
- To improve decision-making under uncertainty, leaders must both work to uncover hidden knowledge and build adaptive, flexible systems for the truly unknown.

Each of these domains demands different tools and temperaments: data and intelligence, intuition and imagination, ethics, and humility. A systems thinker acknowledges that uncertainty is not a flaw, but a fundamental condition of life in complex environments.

The A3 approaches uncertainty through operationalising ethical coherence (Aram), distortion vigilance (Aanavam) and legitimate agency through the pentad of knowledge, action, experience, governance, and absorption (Adhikaram) as a recursive triad. Absorption in Adhikaram enables withdrawal and review.

Critical Systems Thinking (Jackson, 2024)

Jackson's (2024) most recent work on *Critical Systems Thinking* (CST) frames these crises, ecological collapse, geopolitical instability, technological disruption, and social fragmentation as inherently complex, interconnected, and value-laden. CST rejects one-size-fits-all solutions, advocating *methodological pluralism*, *critical attention to power and ethics*, and context-sensitive intervention. In its latest formulation, CST is not limited to diagnosis: it actively integrates major systems methodologies such as the Viable System Model (VSM), Soft Systems Methodology (SSM), and the EPIC framework, enabling the design and execution of interventions that are adaptive, inclusive, and critically aware.

Where **Critical Systems Thinking (CST)** provides a rich integration platform for multi-method intervention in complex crises, the **A3 Model** offers an integrated architecture that embeds ethical coherence, distortion awareness, and agency legitimacy into a continuous, self-adaptive governance loop. CST equips practitioners with the methodologies to navigate and address systemic complexity; A3 ensures that such interventions remain ethically viable, distortion-resilient, and dynamically aligned with systemic fitness over time.

Radical Uncertainty (Kay and King, 2020)

Another relevant influence on this book is the work of leading British economists Kay and King (2020) in their work *Radical Uncertainty*. John Kay and Mervyn King's concept of radical uncertainty challenges traditional economic thinking by rejecting the notion that future events can always be neatly quantified through probability models.

Their collaborative work underscores the fundamental difference between measurable risk, where probabilities can be assigned based on historical data and the profound unpredictability inherent in real-world decision-making. They argue that many of the most consequential moments in economics, business, and policy occur in spaces where prior models fail to predict outcomes because the underlying assumptions do not account for unforeseen variables, emergent dynamics, or unknown unknowns.

Unlike conventional approaches that attempt to reduce uncertainty to quantifiable risk, Kay and King emphasize the importance of flexibility, judgment, and heuristics, simple yet effective rules of thumb that guide decision-making when probabilities are unknowable. They illustrate that in these moments, effective leaders and institutions do not rely solely on predictive analytics but cultivate an adaptive mindset, capable of adjusting strategies as novel situations unfold.

This perspective has wide-ranging implications for financial markets, corporate strategy, and governance, suggesting that overconfidence in models can lead to blind spots that make systems vulnerable to unforeseen shocks such as financial crises, pandemics, or geopolitical disruptions. By embracing radical uncertainty, decision-makers can create more resilient structures that are designed to withstand unpredictable events rather than optimize solely for forecasted scenarios.

Their work reframes our understanding of uncertainty itself, not as a deficiency to be corrected through more precise calculations, but as an inevitable and often defining feature of the complex systems that shape our world.

True uncertainty reveals itself only after all contingencies have been mapped out. We cannot legislate how, when, and where these unknown unknowns will emerge, but we must remain aware that they exist dormant, awaiting activation and engagement.

2.3 Ambiguity

Ambiguity refers to situations where something is unclear, open to multiple interpretations, or lacks a definite meaning. It can exist in language, decision-making, philosophy, or even everyday situations. Let us break it down:

Types of Ambiguity

- **Linguistic Ambiguity** - When a word, phrase, or sentence has multiple meanings.
  - ***Example:*** *"I saw the man with the telescope." Did I see the man using a telescope, or did the man have a telescope?*
- **Situational Ambiguity** - When an event or scenario has multiple explanations.
  - ***Example:*** *In a mystery novel, an event might appear one way but be entirely different upon closer inspection.*
- **Philosophical Ambiguity** - Complex, existential questions that do not have clear answers.
  - ***Example:*** *"What is consciousness?" Different perspectives exist, but no single, universally agreed definition.*
- **Decision-Making Ambiguity** - When uncertainty impacts choices due to lack of full information.
  - ***Example:*** *Business leaders often make decisions with incomplete market data, hoping for the best outcome.*
- **Moral Ambiguity** - where actions, agents, or outcomes admit multiple defensible moral readings, leaving right/wrong indeterminate ex ante or even ex post.

  - ***Example:*** forcing a value tradeoff between public safety and civil liberties under uncertainty.

Why Does Ambiguity Matter?

- **Encourages critical thinking** - Forces deeper analysis rather than accepting information at face value.
- **Drives creativity** - Open-ended situations allow for multiple possibilities and innovations.
- **Influences communication** - Misunderstandings can arise due to vague language or unclear intent.

A3 treats ambiguity as a governance condition, not a failure: Aram specifies ethically coherent aims under indeterminacy, Aanavam diagnoses the uncertainty and distortion that sustain ambiguity, and Adhikaram equips legitimate, option-preserving action that can be revised as evidence and context evolve, turning ambiguity from paralysis into principled, adaptive decisionmaking.

2.4 Complexity

Complexity arises when a system consists of many interconnected elements whose interactions generate emergent outcomes and properties not found in any single element. Complex systems exhibit nonlinearity, self-organization, feedback loops, and sensitivity to initial conditions.

Natural ecosystems, weather patterns, cities, economies, supply chains, and even the human brain are complex. Complexity in human systems also arises from cultural norms, psychological states, historical baggage, and institutional inertia. In such systems, change cannot be forced linearly. It must be guided, nudged, and co-created.

From a Tamil Saiva Siddhantist perspective, complexity manifests when there is disharmony between Aram (virtue/

purpose), Aanavam (ego/illusion), and Adhikaram (capability/agency). Misalignment among these components creates distortion, dysfunction, and suffering. Complexity, then, is not just structural, it is ethical, experiential, and existential.

In this framework, navigating complexity means recognising the sacredness of interconnectedness, the inevitability of emergence, and the need for continuous self-reflection and alignment.

16 Traits of Complexity

Joanna Boehnert's 16 traits (Boehnert, 2018) serve as a conceptual map of complexity's landscape. Rather than viewing a system as a simple sum of its parts, her framework emphasizes that complexity arises from the interwoven tapestry of nonlinearity, feedback, and emergent order. This perspective is invaluable in areas as diverse as economic policy, organizational strategy, ecology, and technology design. By recognizing that each trait interacts with the others, often in unpredictable ways, we learn that linear models and rigid predictions will always fall short. Instead, embracing these traits calls for flexible thinking, resilient structures, and the humility to acknowledge that uncertainty is not a bug, but a defining feature of the world around us.

- **Nonlinearity:** Small causes can lead to disproportionately large effects. The relationships in a complex system rarely follow a straight, predictable line; feedback and multiplicative interactions dominate over simple cause and effect. **Example:** Small causes can lead to outsized effects. A minor code bug in a banking system triggered cascading failures across multiple platforms, causing massive service outages, a textbook case of nonlinear amplification. **A3 lens:** Nonlinearity is feedbacksensitive recursion, where ethical coherence, distortion awareness, and legitimate agency determine whether feedback amplifies fragility or stabilises function.

- **Emergence:** Properties or patterns arise at the system level that cannot be deduced merely from understanding individual parts. These "emergent" phenomena are new qualities that come from the interactions among components. **Example:** Coherent patterns arise from decentralized interactions. Murmurations of starlings, where no bird leads yet all fly in precise synchrony, demonstrate how collective intelligence can emerge without hierarchy. **A3 lens**: Emergence is continuous, feedbacksensitive recursion; Aram (ethical coherence) sets systemlevel aims and guardrails, Aanavam (distortion awareness) surfaces misalignments or biases in local interactions, and Adhikaram (legitimate agency) equips the system to retune couplings and rules so emergent patterns stabilise function rather than amplify risk.
- **Feedback Loops:** Both positive (reinforcing) and negative (balancing) feedback cycles drive complex systems. Such loops can amplify change or work to moderate it, making the system's behaviour extremely sensitive to its current state. **Example:** Processes reinforce (positive) or dampen (negative) changes. Melting polar ice reduces Earth's reflectivity, leading to more heat absorption and faster melting, an accelerating feedback loop in climate systems. **A3 lens:** Ethicsaware signal loops. Aram sets coherent stability aims and guardrails for what the loop should pursue, Aanavam surfaces distortions and harmful couplings

that turn small errors into amplification, and Adhikaram provides the legitimate capability to retune gains, filters, and thresholds so feedback stabilises function rather than amplifies fragility.

- **Adaptation:** Components within complex systems adjust their behaviour in response to local interactions and changing environmental cues. This ongoing adaptation keeps the system in continuous flux as it responds to both internal dynamics and external pressures. **Example:** Systems reorganise to meet new conditions. During the pandemic, many retailers rapidly shifted to ecommerce, reconfigured supply chains, and redeployed staff demonstrating systemic learning and structural flexibility under acute pressure. **A3 lens:** Ethicsdriven structural reconfiguration. *Aram* (ethical coherence) defines the guiding principles for change, *Aanavam* (distortion awareness) identifies maladaptive patterns and bottlenecks, and *Adhikaram* (legitimate agency) ensures the capability to redesign structures and operations, so adaptation serves longterm viability rather than shortterm expediency.
- **Self-Organization:** In the absence of centralised control, order can emerge spontaneously in complex systems through the local interactions of their parts. The system "organises" itself even when no single agent directs the overall behaviour. **Example:** Order arises from decentralised actions. Urban traffic flow patterns often emerge from the collective behaviour of individual drivers adapting to conditions, sometimes matching, or even surpassing the performance of centrally imposed interventions. **A3 lens:** *Recursive agency-fitness alignment. Aram* (ethical coherence)

defines what "fit" means for the system's order, *Aanavam* (distortion awareness) detects misalignments or harmful local rules that compromise global viability, and *Adhikaram* (legitimate agency) provides the capacity to influence local interactions or boundary conditions so selforganization aligns with the system's longterm purpose rather than drifting toward instability or inequity.

- **Interconnectedness:** Every component interacts with many others, meaning that a change in one part of the system can have cascading effects throughout. This web of connections is central to understanding systemic vulnerability and resilience. **Example:** A disruption in one node affects the entire network. A semiconductor shortage in Taiwan triggered delays in automobile production worldwide, revealing the fragility and interdependence of global supply chains. **A3 lens**: *Coherence across Aram-Aanavam-Adhikaram*, the triadic governance loop. *Aram* (ethical coherence) ensures that crosssystem linkages serve the system's intended (ethical) purpose, *Aanavam* (distortion awareness) identifies harmful or unstable interdependencies, and *Adhikaram* (legitimate agency) enables interventions that strengthen resilience and limit cascading failures.
- **Diversity:** Heterogeneity among parts whether in terms of function, structure, or behaviour contributes to a system's overall richness and its capacity to respond to change. Diversity helps buffer the system against shocks and fosters innovative responses. **Example:** Variety enhances resilience. The Amazon rainforest's biodiversity allows it to absorb shocks from

fires and droughts better than monoculture plantations. **A3 lens:** *Aram* (ethical coherence) ensures diversity is maintained and valued as a viability asset, *Aanavam* (distortion awareness) detects homogenisation pressures or biases that erode resilience, and *Adhikaram* (legitimate agency) mobilises capacity to protect and integrate diversity into decisionmaking and system design.

- **Sensitivity to Initial Conditions:** Often described as the "butterfly effect," even minute differences in starting conditions can lead to wildly divergent outcomes. This trait undermines the ability to predict long-term behaviour precisely. **Example:** Tiny differences lead to divergent outcomes. In meteorology, minute variations in early measurements can completely alter the predicted path of a hurricane. **A3 lens**: *Aram* frames preparedness strategies that accept inherent unpredictability, *Aanavam* identifies misperceptions of certainty or overreliance on precise forecasts, and *Adhikaram* equips the system with adaptive capacities to act under scenario variance rather than deterministic assumptions.
- **Distributed Control:** Rather than being governed by a top-down authority, complex systems typically operate under decentralized control. Decision-making is spread out among many agents, each contributing to the emergent order. **Example:** No central authority governs the whole. The internet is governed by protocols shared across networks, making it resilient against single points of failure. **A3 lens:** *Aram* sets shared ethical and operational principles across distributed nodes, *Aanavam* uncovers coordination fail-

ures or misaligned local incentives, and *Adhikaram* provides mechanisms to realign or intervene without undermining decentralisation's benefits.

- **Unpredictability:** Because of the nonlinear interactions, feedback cycles, and sensitivity to initial conditions, the future behaviour of complex systems is inherently difficult to forecast. Uncertainty is not just about lacking data; it is baked into the system's fabric. **Example:** Outcomes defy linear forecasting. Despite sophisticated risk models, financial markets can crash without clear precursors. **A3 lens:** *Aram* grounds decisionmaking in principles that remain valid under uncertainty, *Aanavam* detects flawed assumptions and blind spots in predictive models, and *Adhikaram* ensures legitimate authority to pivot strategies quickly as conditions shift.
- **Context-Dependence:** The behaviour and outcomes of the system are deeply influenced by its environmental context. What works or emerges in one setting might be entirely different in another, emphasizing the role of local conditions and history. **Example:** Outcomes vary with setting. The success of mobile payments in Kenya (e.g., M-Pesa) compared to cash-preferred rural India highlights how context shapes adoption. Although, recent developments indicate a shift in India. **A3 lens:** *Aram* aligns objectives with local values and constraints, *Aanavam* surfaces false generalisations or contextinsensitive rules, and *Adhikaram* legitimises adaptation of strategies and interventions to local realities.
- **Dynamic Interplay:** Components in a complex system are in constant, dynamic interaction. These ongo-

ing exchanges ensure that the system evolves continuously and is not simply a static assemblage of parts. **Example:** Systems are in constant flux, with shifting relationships and balances. This is exemplified by the ongoing negotiations and shifting alliances in coalition governments. **A3 lens:** *Aram* provides stable guiding commitments through change, *Aanavam* detects destructive interaction patterns or emerging misalignments, and *Adhikaram* applies interventions to reshape relationships toward constructive systemic evolution.

- **Scale-Dependence:** Patterns and processes can shift dramatically when observed at different scales. Local interactions may give rise to global phenomena, and similarly, global dynamics can filter down and reshape local behaviours. **Example:** Patterns or rules at one level may not hold at another. The detailed behaviours seen in cellular biology often erratically diverge from what we observe when looking at overall organism health. **A3 lens:** *Aram* ensures coherence of objectives across scales, *Aanavam* identifies scalemismatch distortions (e.g., local optimisation harms global viability), and *Adhikaram* coordinates interventions that align local and global system dynamics.
- **Historical Contingency:** The past matters significantly. The system's current state is the result of its unique historical journey, meaning that understanding its evolution requires looking at the sequence of events that led it there. **Example:** Current states are shaped by unique sequences of past events. Japan's remarkable post-war economic boom was decisively shaped by specific, contingent historical factors that continue

to influence its industrial policies. **A3 lens:** *Aram* respects historically informed constraints and opportunities, *Aanavam* reveals distortions from selective or mythologised history, and *Adhikaram* enables adaptive strategies that integrate historical insight without being locked into path dependency.

- **Robustness and Fragility:** Complex systems often display a paradoxical mix of stability, showing robustness to everyday fluctuations and vulnerability to rare shocks. Systems can be delicately balanced so that routine disturbances are absorbed, while atypical events trigger sudden transitions. **Example:** Resilience to frequent stress does not ensure survival under rare conditions. Coral reefs can withstand repeated wave action but collapse when ocean temperatures rise just slightly beyond threshold. **A3 lens:** *Aram* defines viability boundaries and acceptable risk levels, *Aanavam* detects hidden fragilities masked by apparent robustness, and *Adhikaram* empowers initiative-taking measures that strengthen resilience to rare, highimpact events.
- **Bounded Rationality:** The agents within complex systems operate with limited information and computational abilities. Instead of perfectly optimal decisions, they use heuristics and shortcuts that fit their immediate context, which in turn can drive unexpected system-wide behaviours. **Example:** Decision-makers often act with limited information and use rules-of-thumb. During natural disasters, emergency responders rely on experience-based heuristics rather than perfect data, enabling rapid, life-saving decisions. **A3 lens:** *Aram* frames heuristic use in line with ethical

priorities, *Aanavam* identifies where limited cognition leads to systemic distortion or bias, and *Adhikaram* develops structures and tools that enhance decision quality within bounded capacities.

While complexity science has mapped the patterns that define complex systems, the A3 model uniquely converts these insights into a recursive ethics of design and governance. Rather than treating these traits as merely observational features, A3 builds upon them to create computable grammars of viability providing a practical architecture for diagnosis, ethical alignment, and dynamic intervention across both living and artificial systems. See Appendix A for Table and Reframing Complexity through A3.

Reflections and Recap

Complexity is not a flaw to be fixed, but a reality to engage. VUCA is not a transitional irritation but a condition of deeply interconnected adaptive systems. Navigating complexity requires ethical grounding (*Aram*), self-awareness and distortion diagnosis (*Aanavam*), and authorised, agile agency (*Adhikaram*). Ancient systems like Tamil Saiva Siddhantam offer ontologies and metaphors that deepen contemporary complexity thinking.

True navigation of complexity demands more than adaptability, it requires that systems internalise complexity as part of their ethical fabric, evolving governance recursively rather than reactively. Complexity must not just be managed or survived, but ethically metabolised; A3 is designed to operationalise this ethical metabolism, making viable action possible even under radical uncertainty and ambiguity.

The A3 Model is designed precisely for this systemic necessity. As we transition into the next chapter, we examine the system itself; its structure, behaviour, and the lens of systems thinking that equips us to understand and act within such dynamic realities.

CHAPTER-END REFLECTION PROMPTS

- How comfortable are you with uncertainty, ambiguity, and unpredictability?

- Which trait of complexity do you see most often ignored in your environment?

- What does "ethical metabolism" of complexity look like in practice?

CHAPTER 3: THE SYSTEM

What this Chapter explores: you will be introduced to the foundational principles of systems thinking, with an emphasis on how systems are defined by their purpose, boundaries, and patterns of feedback. Moving beyond conventional models, the chapter integrates insights from Saiva Siddhantam, showing how metaphysical triads such as Pati-Pasu-Pasam and Aram-Aanavam-Adhikaram resonate with and enrich modern systems logic. You will explore how feedback loops - both reinforcing and balancing shape system behaviour over time, and why the concept of "nothingness" (Shunyam/Verumai) offers a generative ontological space for ethical transformation. By the end of the chapter, you will understand systems not as static entities but as living, recursive patterns shaped by both structure and consciousness.

3.1 Systems and Systems Thinking

A system is more than a mere collection of components; it is a cohesive, interdependent structure that generates novel behaviours, functions, and purposes through dynamic interaction. Whether the system is mechanical, biological, social, or conceptual, its identity and function are defined by the relationships among its parts. This inherent relational quality distinguishes a true system from a simple aggregate.

Example: The Car: A vehicle only emerges when the engine, wheels, gearbox, and fuel tank are assembled and interconnected in a meaningful way. Remove or disrupt any component or their interactions, and the system's function is lost.

Feedback Loops

Systems maintain their stability or adapt to new conditions through feedback loops. These mechanisms monitor outcomes and provide corrective responses, underlying biological homeostasis, effective organizational governance, and strategic adaptability.

3.1.1 The Saiva Siddhantam Perspective

In Tamil Saiva Siddhantam, the Pati-Pasu-Paasam triad mirrors this systemic view:

- **Pati:** The Whole (Ground of Being)
- **Pasu:** The Parts or Entities (Bound Agents)
- **Paasam:** The Bonds/Interactions

Aram-Aanavam-Adhikaram is articulated as an ethical-governance grammar. Pati (the Lord or the Whole being) anchors Aram as the ethical centre of gravity, an ordering coherence that orients purpose, right relation, and measure; Aram thus names the lived consonance with Pati's truth. Pasu (the bound soul) is enmeshed in Pasam (the bonds), from which ethical distortion arises: Pasam is classically *karma*, *aanavam*, and *maya* which generates drift, opacity, and misalignment; this is the root of Aanavam as distortion vigilance, the signal of deviation from Aram that demands diagnosis and correction.

Adhikaram, legitimate agency, names the qualified capacity to act toward restoration; in the Meykandar tradition as elaborated by Arunandi Sivam, this fitness is recursively constituted by a pentad: Knowledge (contextual understanding), Action (ethically gated execution), Experience (discernment through outcomes), Governance (legitimacy gating and oversight), and Absorption (deep learning that integrates lived narratives and emergent conditions).

Together, these map the soteriological logic of Pati-Pasu-Pasam into a practical framework for ethical coherence (Aram), distortion recognition and restraint (Aanavam), and rightly empowered agency (Adhikaram), with Tirumantiram and Tirukkural furnishing foundational poetic and practical aphorisms that sustain this moral ontology.

The Tirukkural, by Tiruvalluvar, frames everyday virtue, governance, and love in civic aphorisms that resonate with ethical purpose and legitimacy. Tirumular's Tirumantiram deepens the symbolic grammar of Pati-Pasu-Pasam, providing poetic guidance for ethical vigilance (Aanavam) and spiritual consonance (Aram). This synthesis bridges metaphysical principle with practical agency in the A3 Model.

3.1.2 Flourishing and Nothingness

Ancient Tamil systemic wisdom teaches that true flourishing does not arise from conquest, accumulation, or static optimization, but from the system's capacity for continuous absorption, ethical realignment, and adaptive transformation. It is not strength, but suppleness *and unceasing openness to evolve in alignment with deeper truths* that ensures lasting coherence and vitality.

At the heart of this philosophy lies the concept of "nothingness" not as nihilism or absence, but as a dynamic potentiality. In Tamil Saiva metaphysics, nothingness is the fertile void that precedes creation, the sacred pause before emergence, the space where ego dissolves and new relational order can arise. It signifies the courage to let go of rigid identity, obsolete structures, or unexamined beliefs, thereby making room for renewal, insight, and system-wide innovation.

This view contrasts sharply with Western models of optimization, which often treat systems as instruments to be perfected. Tamil thought invites us instead to consider emptiness as an ethical and epistemological gesture, a systemic clearing that allows emergence, learning, and the deep re-patterning of relationships.

This theme will be expanded in the *A3 Manifesto*, where nothingness becomes a generative principle for ethical recursion, disruptive insight, and the design of living, evolving systems. In a world overburdened by noise, complexity, and control, the wisdom of letting go becomes not only philosophically profound but vital.

3.2 Defining a System: Key Properties

A system:

- Comprises interconnected elements or entities.
- Is structured for a purpose or function.
- Produces outcomes greater than the sum of its parts.
- Maintains coherence and stability through feedback mechanisms.

- Engages with its environment receiving inputs, producing outputs.

This way of understanding systems frames complexity as dynamic, adaptive, and unpredictable. Systems are not fixed blueprints: they learn, evolve, and sometimes collapse.

3.3 Systems Thinking

Systems thinking is both a discipline and a perspective. It urges us to see wholes, patterns, and relationships rather than isolated events, preferring synthesis over analysis, context over content, and patterns over single snapshots.

> *"A framework for seeing interconnections in a system and a discipline for seeing and understanding the whole system and the structures that underlie complex situations."*
> *–UK Civil Service Guidelines (2022)*

3.3.1 Practical Applications

Systems thinking aids in:

- Understanding systemic function and behaviour.
- Identifying causal loops, delays, and unintended consequences.
- Navigating complexity without reductionism.
- Designing interventions for both short-term and long-term outcomes.

3.3.2 Key Components

- **Entities:** Individual elements with attributes and capacities.

- **Relationships:** Interactions among entities that define the system's character.
- **Feedback Loops:** Mechanisms for self-regulation and adaptation.
- **Boundaries:** The scope within which the system is analysed.
- **Environment:** The external world with which the system interacts.
- **Purpose and Function:** The intended outcomes or roles the system fulfils.

A Tamil perspective further enriches these components by emphasizing ethical considerations (Aram), ontological reflection (Aanavam), and legitimate agency (Adhikaram).

3.4 Systems Mapping

Systems mapping is a visual method to depict the structure and dynamics of systems, facilitating understanding and intervention design.

3.4.1 What Systems Mapping Helps Identify

- Entities and stakeholders
- Relationships and flows
- Causal and feedback loops
- Power dynamics and leverage points
- Temporal or spatial dimensions

Maps can take various forms: causal loop diagrams, stock and flow models, network graphs. No map is fully complete, as systems are partly unknowable and often observer-dependent. Instead, mapping is an iterative process, one that evolves as insight deepens.

The A3 model's diagnostic dashboard encourages mapping from both observer and participant perspectives, acknowledging the embeddedness and subjectivity of all actors. This duality is key to authentic systemic insight.

3.5. Systems, Systems Thinking, and Complexity: An Overview

Systems thinking is deeply intertwined with complexity science. Both recognize that:

- Parts cannot be fully understood in isolation.
- Relationships shape outcomes.
- Interventions create ripple effects.
- Purpose and function are emergent and dynamic.

A minor change in one part of a governance system (for example, a governance policy) can have far-reaching social, institutional, and even technological effects. The human body reacts similarly: a localised inflammation might affect mood, energy, and cognition. While systems thinking connects these dots, complexity thinking reminds us to beware of linear, simplistic expectations.

Systems are open, they exchange information, energy, and matter with their environment. They evolve over time and contain nested sub-systems (e.g., organs in bodies, teams in organisations). They have multiple identities and feedback mechanisms. Understanding them requires both detail and distance.

The Tamil Saiva tradition contributes richly to this view. The alignment of Pati (purpose/wholeness), Pasu (entity/identity), and Paasam (relationships/attachments) forms a systemic ethic. When these elements misalign: when Aanavam clouds vision, or Aram is abandoned, instability and complexity arise.

Table: *Comparison of foundational principles in Classical (Western) Systems Thinking and Tamil Saiva Siddhantam, illustrating distinct approaches to boundaries, feedback, agency, and purpose.*

Conceptual Axis	Classical Systems Thinking	Tamil Saiva Siddhantam (Relational Real) A3
System Boundary	Observerdefined operational/functional boundaries	Ethical and ontological
System Components	Entities, processes, and functions	Pati (source), Pasu (agent), Paasam (relation)
Feedback Mechanism	Reinforcing (positive) and balancing (negative) feedback loops	Recursion through Aram, Aanavam and Adhikaram
Purpose	Viability, homeostasis, or optimization (contextdependent)	Realisation of ethical coherence (Aram)
Agency/ Fitness	External performance criteria	Legitimate action (Adhikaram) through alignment
Distortion	Noise, error, drift	Aanavam - egoic closure and systemic entropy
Recursion/ Structure	Organisational recursion (e.g., VSM's recursive viable functions; nested viable units)	Ethicalontological recursion via Aram-Aanavam-Adhikaram shaping perception, purpose, and intervention.

3.6. The Philosophical Foundations of Systems Thinking

Deep systems thinking is fundamentally philosophical and engages six interwoven dimensions:

a. Epistemology

How do we know what we know?

In systems thinking, epistemology is essential because it challenges us to reflect on the source and validity of our knowledge. Systems are multifaceted, and knowledge about them comes from a blend of empirical data, experiential insights, and often tacit understandings. This means that instead of relying solely on quantifiable data or linear models, the systems thinker must appreciate that information is gathered through diverse perspectives such as scientific inquiry, historical context, and even the collective wisdom of a community. Recognizing the limitations of our own knowledge encourages a more humble and adaptable approach, wherein multiple viewpoints and methods are synthesized to form a more comprehensive picture of a system's behaviour.

b. Ontology

What is the nature of being, identity, and agency?

When applied to systems thinking, ontology compels us to define what exactly constitutes a system. Are systems merely aggregates of independent parts, or do their unique, interwoven interactions give rise to an entity with properties that are irreducible to its components? Ontological inquiry asks us to reexamine traditional boundaries; it suggests that a system's identity and behaviour arise not only from its parts but also from the relationships, interdependencies, and even emergent properties that these interactions produce. In considering systems from an ontological perspective, designers and analysts are challenged to look beyond reductionist models and embrace the holistic nature of systems, where relationships and context play as much of a role in defining being as the isolated components themselves.

c. Logic

What structures reasoning and causality?

Logic provides the framework within which we understand causality, infer relationships, and structure our thinking. Yet, the logic that underpins systems thinking must move beyond linear cause-and-effect reasoning. In complex systems, causality is often circular rather than straight-line feedback loops, interdependencies, and non-linear interactions demand a more sophisticated mode of reasoning that accounts for simultaneous, multi-directional influences. This dynamic logic is crucial for constructing models that faithfully represent the mutable and often paradoxical nature of real-world systems. It also challenges us to continuously refine our hypotheses and models, ensuring that our reasoning remains flexible in the face of emerging data and shifting systemic behaviour.

d. Ethics

What constitutes right action, wise design, or just governance?

Ethics in systems thinking invites us to consider what constitutes just and responsible action when engaging with complex, interrelated systems. Decisions made within these systems often have far-reaching consequences, not just for a single component but for entire networks of relationships. By integrating ethical thinking, systems minds are encouraged to prioritize long-term sustainability, equity, and the well-being of all stakeholders. Whether designing public policy, organizational structures, or technology systems, an ethical framework ensures that decisions are not solely driven by efficiency or profit, but also by the values of fairness, justice, and care for the common good. This ethical lens is especially potent in today's interconnected world, where one decision in a complex system can spark unforeseen ripple effects across social, economic, and ecological domains.

e. Forms

How do concepts, categories, and models shape our perceptions?

The concept of forms deals with how our cognitive models - abstract representations, categories, and diagrams shape our understanding of complex systems. These forms are indispensable tools for simplification and communication: they allow us to distil vast, messy realities into coherent models and frameworks. However, this process of abstraction also introduces biases and limitations. The forms we use invariably emphasize some elements while neglecting others, potentially obscuring important nuances. By scrutinizing our own modes of representation, systems thinkers are prompted to remain critically aware that the maps we create are not the territory itself. An expanded exploration of forms pushes us to continually re-evaluate and refine our models so that they evolve in tandem with our understanding of the systems they are intended to describe.

f. First Principles

What are the irreducible foundations of our thought systems?

First principles are the irreducible assumptions or fundamental truths upon which our entire system of thinking is built. This dimension of philosophy encourages us to strip away layers of complexity and conventional wisdom to reach the core of our questions. In systems thinking, engaging with first principles means questioning the basic assumptions behind our models, policies, or design choices. It is a call for innovation by challenging established norms and peeling back the layers of accumulated knowledge, we often discover novel insights and solutions. First principles thinking is transformative because it not only disrupts complacency but also lays a foundation for building new frameworks that are better aligned with the emergent realities of complex systems.

These philosophical axes are not abstract; they inform everything from organizational design to AI development and social movement response. Their interplay underpins authentic, effective systems thinking.

In Saiva Siddhantam, the Pati – Pasu – Paasam first principle sets the platform to explore how the philosophical underpinnings provide shape to Ethical Coherence, Adaptable Legitimate Agency and mitigating Systemic Distortion.

3.7 Closing Reflection

Systems are all around us: from our bodies and organisations, from algorithms to ecosystems. To truly navigate complexity, we must learn to see, feel, and act systemically.

By integrating traditional wisdom, ethical insight, and contemporary theory, we can build not only better systems but more aligned and humane ones. The next chapter will delve into theoretical discourses, holism, reductionism, worldviews, and interpretive paradigms that shape how we understand and apply systems thinking

CHAPTER-END REFLECTION PROMPTS

- Do you think of systems as mechanical or living? How does that affect your decisions?

- How does the Aram - Aanavam - Adhikaram triad reframe your understanding of feedback and change?

- What obsolete structures are you (or your institution) afraid to let go of?

CHAPTER 4: **DISCOURSES IN SYSTEMS**

What this Chapter explores: *you will critically examine a range of systems discourses, including holism, critical theory, interpretive paradigms, and governance frameworks such as ESG. You will learn how worldviews shape the very foundations of institutional design, influencing what is seen, valued, and acted upon within complex systems. The chapter explores tensions between reductionism and emergence, rationalism, and pluralism, and shows how these tensions manifest in real-world decision-making. Drawing from both Western and non-Western epistemologies, you will engage with the concept of plural translation, the ability to move between paradigms without collapsing them, emerging with the insight that system viability requires not uniformity, but ethical coherence across differences.*

Discourses in Systems

To truly appreciate systems thinking and the challenges posed by complex environments, we must consider the dominant theoretical debates. These debates help us understand not only how complex systems work but also how different perspectives influence our analysis and decision-making. In other words, while no single theory can capture the full breadth of complexity, knowing the core differences between ideas helps us navigate ambiguity and uncertainty better. The A3 Model builds upon this plurality by offering a triadic, recursive architecture of Aram (ethics), Aanavam (distortion), and Adhikaram (agency) that does not erase these differences but integrates them into a dynamic, ethical system of transformation.

4.1 Holism and Reductionism

4.1.1 Holistic Thinking

Core Idea: Holism is the approach that stresses that the whole is greater than the sum of its parts. In complex, interconnected environments, emergent properties arise from the interplay among components; these features may not be evident if you study individual parts in isolation.

Key Characteristics:

- **Interdependency:** Every element in a system influences and is influenced by others. For example, in an organization, employee morale, leadership style, and corporate culture together determine overall performance; none of which can be fully understood on their own.
- **Emergence:** New properties or behaviours appear from the interaction of components. Think of flocking behaviour in birds: no single bird "contains" the pattern of the flock.

- **Dynamic & Context-Dependent:** A holistic view accepts that changes in one part of the system may create unexpected effects elsewhere. This leads to a need for adaptive strategies that consider the entire network of relationships.

Real-World Example: Consider the healthcare system. Instead of diagnosing a patient by looking at only one symptom, holistic doctors consider lifestyle, diet, mental health, and the environment. This broader view often uncovers patterns such as stress impacting digestion and leads to a more effective, integrative treatment strategy.

Implications in Systems Thinking: A holistic approach helps leaders and decision-makers grasp the "big picture" and plan interventions that account for interconnected feedback loops rather than isolated fixes.

4.1.2 Reductionism

Core Idea: Reductionism seeks to explain a complex phenomenon by breaking it down into its constituent parts. The idea is that if you understand every small element and the rules that govern them, you can reconstruct the behaviour of the entire system.

Key Characteristics:

Dissection and Analysis: Focuses on studying separate components in a controlled, often static, manner.

- **Cause-and-Effect:** Works well when cause-effect relationships are clear. For instance, in mechanical engineering, if a car engine fails, technicians isolate and assess each subsystem (like the fuel system, spark plugs, or cooling system) to identify the problem.

- **Predictability:** Suited for systems where parts behave in predictable, linear ways. Many scientific experiments operate on reductionist principles to evaluate hypotheses and control variables.

Real-World Example: In medicine, reductionism is reflected in the approach taken by many specialists: for example, a cardiologist focusing solely on heart function or an endocrinologist zeroing in on hormonal imbalances. Each discipline isolates aspects of a patient's health to develop a precise treatment.

Implications in Systems Thinking: Reductionist methods provide detailed insight into individual processes. However, in overly complex systems, the challenge is that interactions among parts may lead to non-linear and unpredictable outcomes that reductionism alone cannot explain.

4.2 Systemic vs. Systematic Thinking

4.2.1 Systemic Thinking

Core Idea: Systemic thinking is all about understanding the relationships and interactions that give rise to the properties of the entire system. It is a dynamic, context-bound approach where change is expected and can have non-linear consequences.

Key Characteristics:

- **Interconnectedness and Feedback:** Every action or change often results in feedback loops that modify the system. A small marketing tweak might trigger a significant change in consumer behaviour through social networks.
- **Emergence and Unpredictability:** Because the parts are highly interactive, properties such as stability or in-

stability emerge in ways that cannot be deduced from analysing parts separately.

- **Adaptive and Non-Linear:** The outcomes in systemic systems are often sensitive to initial conditions (think the butterfly effect), which means that small variations can lead to significant differences in behaviour.

Real-World Example: Consider the global financial system. A tiny policy change in one country can ripple through international markets, causing widespread, sometimes unforeseen, economic effects. Systemic thinking prepares managers to anticipate such ripple effects and build resilient systems.

Implications: Leaders who adopt systemic thinking are prepared to manage complexity by recognizing patterns rather than isolated incidents. This is crucial for long-term strategy, especially in dynamic, unpredictable environments.

4.2.2 Systematic Thinking

Core Idea: Systematic thinking involves methodically breaking down a system into a series of defined, sequential steps. It is often used for tasks where the process is repeatable, and outcomes are measurable.

Key Characteristics:

- **Step-by-Step Analysis:** It employs structured methods such as process mapping or algorithmic analysis.
- **Predictability and Control:** The focus is on creating order through linear steps that are traceable and repeatable.
- **Objectivity:** Systematic thinking minimizes subjectivity by focusing on clearly measurable variables.

Real-World Example: In project management, a systematic approach might involve using detailed Gantt charts and predefined tasks to ensure that a project follows a set trajectory. This method works well in environments where variables are well known and controlled.

Implications: While systematic thinking is excellent for processes that require a consistent, analytical approach, it might fall short in dealing with the unpredictability and emergent properties of complex, interconnected systems.

Systemic vs. Systematic Thinking – Comparison Table

Dimension	Systemic Thinking	Systematic Thinking
Core orientation	Interconnected, relational, whole-systems perspective	Linear, stepwise, process-driven perspective
Primary aim	Understand patterns, feedback, and emergent behaviour	Achieve repeatable, controlled outcomes via defined steps
Causality model	Circular causality; multi-directional influences	Linear causality; input→process→output
Context assumption	Dynamic, evolving, context-dependent	Stable, well-bounded, controllable
Treatment of complexity	Embraces nonlinearity, interdependence, uncertainty	Reduces complexity into manageable sequences
Feedback use	Central: reinforcing and balancing loops guide adaptation	Typically end-of-stage checks and milestones
Sensitivity to initial conditions	High - minor changes can cascade	Low-moderate variation constrained by procedure
Typical tools	Causal loop diagrams, stock-flow models, network maps, scenarios	SOPs, checklists, flowcharts, Gantt charts, stage-gates

Dimension	Systemic Thinking	Systematic Thinking
Strengths	Reveals interdependencies; anticipates ripple effects; builds resilience	Ensures consistency, quality control, accountability, efficiency
Limitations	Harder to standardise; requires judgement and iteration	Can miss emergence; vulnerable to out-of-scope risks
Best-fit problems	Wicked socio-technical issues; policy; ecosystems; markets	Well-defined processes; compliance; manufacturing; projects
Example (pandemic)	Integrates health-economy-education-equity; adapts to feedback	Defines testing, ICU, procurement, lockdown procedures
Governance cadence	Continuous sensing, learning, and course correction	Periodic reviews; staged approvals; checkpoints
Error handling	Detects/dampens systemic failure modes and unintended effects	Corrects deviations from plan/specification
Role of metrics	Portfolio: leading/lagging, cross-domain indicators	Focused KPIs aligned to process steps
People and power	Surfaces stakeholder dynamics, incentives, positionalities	Clarifies roles, responsibilities, handoffs
Change approach	Probe-sense-respond; iterative reframing	Plan-do-check-act; controlled implementation
Knowledge stance	Multi-perspectival, reflexive, context-aware	Objective, standardised, procedure-focused
When to combine	Use systemic to frame and de-risk; use systematic to execute	Use systematic to deliver; use systemic to anticipate/ adapt

Case Illustration: Systemic vs. Systematic Thinking in Pandemic Response

The Systematic Approach

Early in the COVID-19 crisis, many governments adopted a systematic approach. This included defining case thresholds, imposing lockdowns, expanding ICU capacity, and procuring ventilators. These sequential, rule-based steps were essential for immediate containment, but they primarily addressed the virus as a biomedical problem.

Seeing the Systemic Picture

A systemic lens, by contrast, revealed a host of hidden ripple effects:

- School closures disrupted child nutrition programs.
- Domestic violence hotlines saw surges in calls.
- Supply-chain shocks led to empty shelves in some regions, while food went to waste in others.
- Mental health crises rose sharply, particularly among youth.

Integrating Systemic and Systematic Thinking

Jurisdictions that combined systematic protocols with systemic awareness fared better.

New Zealand, for example, paired strict border controls with rapid income-support measures, culturally tailored messaging for Māori and Pasifika communities, and clear daily briefings that fostered social trust. By acknowledging feedback loops among health, economics, and social cohesion, leaders minimized long-term damage and maintained public legitimacy.

Key Lesson

Systematic actions provide essential structure and order. However, systemic insight prevents collateral fragmentation and enables adaptive, mid-course corrections that are vital in complex, evolving crises like a pandemic.

4.3 Perspectives, Paradigms and Worldviews

4.3.1 Worldview

Core Idea: Worldview refers to the deep-seated, often long-lasting, belief system shaped by culture, religion, education, and life experiences. It forms a stable framework through which individuals interpret life and meaning.

Key Characteristics:

- **Enduring Beliefs:** These are constant and not easily changed by temporary conditions. For example, a person's ethical or religious principles often remain steady despite situational pressures.
- **Cultural and Moral Foundations:** Worldview helps determine what one considers right or wrong, influencing decisions at a fundamental level.
- **Examples in Practice:** An executive who has a deeply ingrained belief in transparency might prioritize ethical practices consistently, whereas someone with a different worldview might justify confidentiality over full disclosure even during crises.

4.3.2 Perspective

Core Idea: Perspective is more situational; it is a person's point of view at a particular moment in time. It is shaped by immediate experiences, contexts, and conditions.

Key Characteristics:

- **Fluid and Context-Dependent:** Unlike worldview, perspective can shift rapidly depending on one's present situation. For instance, during a crisis, someone's perspective on risk may change dramatically.
- **Tactical Decision Making:** Perspective provides immediate guidance and can lead to different conclusions even among people with similar worldviews based on temporary conditions.
- **Interplay Between Them:** While your worldview provides a long-term, stable framework, your perspective may temporarily adjust your approach to problems. Leaders must be aware that while strategic values (worldview) remain constant, tactical approaches (perspective) can and should change as the environment shifts.

For example, two public health officials may both hold a worldview that prioritizes social equity. However, during a pandemic, one operating in an under-resourced rural district might advocate for mobile clinics as an immediate priority, while the other, situated in a dense urban setting, may focus on digital access and communication strategies. Their perspectives are shaped by their local system dynamics, even as their underlying values remain aligned.

The A3 framework interprets such divergence not as conflict, but as a natural expression of *Aanavam*, the contextual and perspectival distortions that arise when shared values meet differing systemic realities. By holding *Aram* (ethical coherence) as the constant setpoint, A3 ensures both officials remain aligned on purpose, while making the distortion visible without delegitimising either view. Through *Adhikaram* (legitimate agency), the framework empowers each to act within their local context, while maintaining a recursive dialogue that allows strategies to adapt and inform one another. In this way, A3 sustains ethical unity across diverse responses, turning variation into a source of systemic resilience rather than fragmentation.

4.3.3 Paradigms

Paradigms function as invisible architectures of thought. They are the shared assumptions, values, and conceptual filters that inform how we define problems, evaluate evidence, and enact solutions. As Kuhn argued, paradigms frame not only what we see but what we consider thinkable.

Worldviews are deeper still. They encompass a society's implicit understanding of what exists, what matters, and what is possible. While paradigms may shift in a generation, worldviews often span centuries, encoded in language, ritual, myth, and institutional norms.

In systems work, paradigms, and worldviews shape:

- How systems are framed and bounded
- What constitutes evidence or authority
- Whose voices are included or excluded
- What kinds of interventions are considered legitimate

For instance, a developmental economist rooted in a growth-oriented paradigm may view a forest primarily as a resource. An Indigenous worldview, in contrast, may see the forest as kin, community, and teacher. Each perspective carries distinct system implications.

The A3 model resists homogenisation. It is designed to surface and hold multiple ontologies and epistemologies in dialogue. Aram (ethical orientation), Aanavam (self-conception), and Adhikaram (agency or power) are not fixed categories, they are interpreted differently across cultures, institutions, and paradigms. The work is not to define a universal standard but to cultivate reflexive alignment within a particular context.

4.4 Interpretive Lenses and Positionality

All knowledge is situated. No observation is free from context. Every system map, policy framework, or AI algorithm is shaped by the biases, intentions, and limitations of its creators. Recognising this is not a weakness, it is a gateway to deeper insight and ethical responsibility.

Interpretive lenses: feminist, ecological, decolonial, critical race, theological reveal the assumptions and absences within dominant systemic models. They ask different questions, foreground different values, and seek different outcomes. A feminist lens, for example, might prioritise care, embodiment, and relational accountability. An Indigenous lens might centre ancestral knowledge, collective agency, and land-based **wisdom.**

Case Illustration: Systems Thinking and Algorithmic Hiring Bias

Interpretive lenses are not abstract ideals; they are essential tools for navigating real-world complexity. Consider the case of AI-driven hiring tools:

4.4.1 Functionalist and Systematic Perspectives

Many organizations adopted algorithmic systems to screen résumés and rank applicants, anticipating improved efficiency and objectivity. From a functionalist or systematic standpoint, these tools were treated as logical optimizers: faster, cheaper, and more consistent than traditional human judgment.

4.4.2 Critical and Feminist Insights

However, when examined through feminist and critical race lenses, these technologies revealed significant hidden problems:

- **Gender Bias:** Systems routinely ranked male-coded résumés higher than female-coded ones.
- **Structural Exclusion:** Candidates from certain universities or ethnic backgrounds were filtered out.
- **Historical Injustice:** In one high-profile instance, an AI penalized applicants from women's colleges, not by design, but because historical hiring patterns encoded discriminatory practices into the data the algorithm learned from.

From a feminist lens, the system failed to account for care-based labour, part-time work related to parenting, or employment gaps; realities disproportionately affecting women yet undervalued by the model. From a critical race perspective, the algorithm reinforced white-majority hiring norms under the banner of "merit."

4.4.3 The Power of Interpretive Lenses

By applying these interpretive frameworks, organizations moved beyond simply asking for greater accuracy from their AI tools. Instead, they confronted the deeper, embedded epistemologies questioning what their systems truly valued and whose interests they served.

The reframed conversation became:

Not just "How do we make this system more accurate?" but rather,

"What kind of system are we building and whom does it include, exclude, or disadvantage?"

This structure elevates the practical and ethical importance of interpretive lenses and systems thinking for contemporary challenges in digital governance and organizational practice.

The A3 model is built on the recognition that all system design emerges from positionality. AEVT, the diagnostic method embedded in A3, explicitly tracks ethical variance not just across actions and outcomes, but across interpretive frames. By surfacing how Aanavam (distortion or misalignment) appears differently through ecological, feminist, or Indigenous lenses, A3 helps organizations avoid premature closure. Rather than suppressing pluralism, it uses it as fuel for deeper ethical coherence.

4.5 Functionalism vs. Social Interpretivism

4.5.1 Functionalism

- **Core Idea:** Functionalism views society (or any complex system) as a set of interrelated parts working together like a living organism. Each part or institution serves a specific function that contributes to the overall stability and health of the system.
- **Key Characteristics:**
    - **Social Order:** Emphasizes that institutions (e.g., government, education, family) exist because they fulfil necessary roles.
    - **Interdependence:** Every component, whether it is a social norm, role, or organization, is critical to maintaining the system's balance.
- **Example in Context:** In an organization, the HR department might be seen as essential for maintaining workforce stability, while the sales department drives

revenue. Each is seen as a crucial "organ" within the greater "body" of the company.

- **Implications:** Applying a functionalist lens encourages leaders to identify each component's role and ensure that they contribute effectively to the overall mission.

4.5.2 Social Interpretivism

- **Core Idea:** Social interpretivism (or interpretivism) argues that meaning is constructed subjectively through human interactions. There is no single "objective" reality; instead, reality is interpreted differently by different people based on their experiences and cultural backgrounds.
- **Key Characteristics:**
    - **Subjective Understanding:** Truth is seen as relative, informed by personal interpretations and interactions.
    - **Cultural and Contextual Sensitivity:** It highlights the importance of understanding context when analysing behaviour or social norms.
- **Example in Context:** In a workplace setting, how a policy is received may depend heavily on the varying interpretations of employees. One group may view a new performance metric as empowering, while another might see it as invasive, even if the policy is factually the same.
- **Implications:** This approach encourages open communication and sensitivity to diverse opinions. In management, it means that policies should be flexible enough to accommodate different interpretations and experiences.

4.6 Critical Theory

- **Core Idea:** Critical theory, with roots in the Frankfurt School, challenges established power structures and ideologies. It emphasizes that facts cannot be separated from the values and social contexts that shape them.
- **Key Characteristics:**
    - **Ideological Analysis:** It analyses how cultural and ideological forces maintain social inequality or control.
    - **Transformative Agenda:** Critical theory is not just about understanding the world, it also advocates for change, questioning dominant paradigms and pushing for a more just society.
- **Example in Context:** A critical theorist might examine a company's policies not only to identify inefficiencies but also to understand how those policies reinforce existing power dynamics. For example, if decision-making is centralized in a way that marginalizes frontline employees, critical theory would question whether this structure perpetuates inequality and stifles innovation.
- **Implications:** For systems leaders, critical theory provides a lens through which to question and potentially reform traditional structures, ensuring that change is informed both by data and by ethical considerations regarding fairness and equity.

Case Illustration: Critical Theory in Corporate ESG Reporting

Many multinational firms now publish annual **ESG (Environmental, Social, Governance)** reports brimming with charts, metrics, and glossy photos. From a surface perspective, these documents signal transparency and responsibility. Yet a **critical-theory lens** asks: *Who defines the metrics? Whose voices are missing? What power dynamics underlie "acceptable" targets?*

A 2023 study of global mining companies showed that while carbon-offset projects were highlighted, Indigenous land-rights conflicts were relegated to footnotes. Community consultations were reported as "completed" even when they relied on translation services that local elders distrusted. The ESG narrative thus reproduced shareholder legitimacy while marginalizing frontline communities.

Activist-researchers used critical discourse analysis to expose this asymmetry. Their findings pressured one firm to add Indigenous representatives to its board-level sustainability committee and to adopt **"free, prior, and informed consent"** as a binding standard shifting decision-making power, not just disclosure language.

Lesson: Critical theory reframes ESG from image management to power redistribution, ensuring that "sustainability" initiatives do not entrench the very inequities they claim to solve.

Note: This case draws from a composite of real reports, discourse analyses, and activist research in ESG contexts. While the specific 2023 study is illustrative, it integrates findings across multiple sources (e.g., Schueth, 2003; Milne & Gray, 2013; Caradonna et al., 2022) to protect anonymity and emphasize thematic clarity.

CST reframes how we select and combine responses across methods and power contexts, while A3 reimagines how systems enact response continuously by hardwiring ethics (Aram), distortion vigilance (Aanavam), and legitimate agency (Adhikaram) into the recursive dynamics themselves. In A3, these functions are intrinsic, inloop operators within the feedback architecture of a system whereas CST primarily orchestrates multimethod diagnosis and intervention with pluralist, reflective governance, and generally locates ethics and legitimacy at the level of methodology choice, boundary critique, and stakeholder inclusion rather than as runtime control parameters.

4.7 Synthesis: Reconciling Multiple Approaches

While these theories might seem to stand in opposition, holism versus reductionism, systemic versus systematic, objective versus subjective, effective systems thinking requires blending these approaches. Consider the following points:

- **Integrated Analysis:** A comprehensive strategy often starts with reductionist methods to identify specific issues, then adopts a holistic or systemic lens to understand the interdependencies that might amplify these issues.
- **Complementary Insights:** Functionalism provides a clear picture of roles and functions, while interpretivism ensures that human experiences, biases, and cultural contexts are not ignored. In practice, this means you not only ask, "What does each part do?" but also "How do people feel about and interpret these roles?"
- **Contextual Judgment:** Recognizing that your immediate perspective might shift in a crisis (versus your long-standing worldview), systems practitioners can adjust tactical approaches while maintaining strategic consistency.

- **Iterative Learning:** In complex systems, leaders must be prepared to cycle between these perspectives as new data emerge. For example, in managing a global supply chain, one may use systematic protocols for daily operations while also using systemic thinking to prepare for disruptive events that change how all parts of the chain interact.

In Saiva Siddhantam, the idea of Gnanam (realised wisdom) reflects this interior alignment. One's perception of reality is shaped by one's level of consciousness, clarity, and ethical attunement. The same system can look different depending on the maturity and alignment of the observer. This offers a profound frame for reflexivity in systemic practice.

A3 and Systems Discourse: *metamapping between dominant systems perspectives and A3's specific governance response*

Perspective	**Key Insight**	**A3 Response**
Holism	Whole is more than the sum of parts	Recognises emergence through recursive coordination (*Aram-Aanavam-Adhikaram* across scales)
Reductionism	Causal analysis of constituent parts	Diagnoses systemic distortion via *Aanavam* as recursive entropy
Interpretive	Meaning is context-bound	Aram frames ethical interpretive coherence
Functionalist	Systems serve stabilizing roles	A3 emphasizes legitimate agency via Adhikaram
Critical Theory	Power, ideology, emancipation	A3 models systemic distortion, collapse, and recovery (Shunyam Protocol)

Perspective	Key Insight	A3 Response
Reflexive/Meta	Observer is embedded	A3 is fully reflexive and triadic, transcending dualist frames

This table maps major systems perspectives to their key insight and the specific A3 governance response, highlighting how A3 operationalises each lens through triadic recursion.

4.8 The Challenge of Translation

Systems thinking aspires to integration, yet this integration often falters at the edges where disciplines, cultures, and languages meet. Translation is not just a technical task; it is an act of deep listening and mutual respect.

Many knowledge systems resist being rendered into technocratic language. Traditional ecological knowledge, spiritual cosmologies, and ethical philosophies may lose meaning when abstracted into KPIs, metrics, or policy briefs. The task of translation, then, is to honour essence while enabling understanding.

True translation involves:

- Contextual sensitivity
- Ontological humility
- Narrative competence
- Willingness to preserve ambiguity when needed

The A3 model was conceived as a translational bridge, a heuristic that allows concepts to move between philosophical, operational, and experiential registers. It does not flatten difference but creates a space where difference becomes generative.

4.9 Closing Reflection

Discourses in systems are not peripheral, they are foundational. The way we see determines the way we act. Holism, paradigms, lenses, and translation are not intellectual luxuries but vital disciplines for navigating the complexity of our time.

We live in systems shaped by invisible logics. To transform them, we must surface these logics, question them, and align them with ethical clarity and collective purpose.

While classical Systems Thinking offers critical insights into holism and complexity, and Interpretive Systems Thinking invites sensitivity to meaning-making and boundary critique, neither fully resolves the need for an embedded, living ethics that evolves dynamically with systemic realities.

The A3 Model synthesizes these dimensions, systemic rigor, interpretive flexibility, and ethical recursion into a living architecture of complexity navigation and transformation.

It is not a balancing act between systemic and interpretive thought; it is their evolutionary unfolding toward systemic ethical renewal.

In the next chapter, we bring these discourses into synthesis through the A3 model: a systems and ethics framework that integrates ancient insight with contemporary strategy, offering a path forward through complexity, agency, and transformation.

CHAPTER-END REFLECTION PROMPTS

- Which systems lens - holistic, interpretive, critical dominates in your field? Is it sufficient?

- How do your own assumptions or positionalities influence what you consider "viable"?

- Can systems be translated across paradigms without distortion?

- How do I balance a detailed analysis of problems with a broader understanding of interconnected factors?

- In what ways do my deeply held beliefs (worldview) influence my day-to-day decision-making?

- Am I open enough to different interpretations (perspectives) to adjust dynamically as situations change

- How can I apply both functionalist insights and interpretivist sensitivity to foster a workplace that is both organized and creative?

- Does my current leadership framework allow for questioning of authority and established norms as encouraged by critical theory?

CHAPTER 5: INTRODUCING THE A3 MODEL – A NEW ORDER OF ETHICAL SYSTEMIC INTELLIGENCE

What this Chapter explores: *In this chapter, you are introduced more formally to the A3 Model - a triadic, recursive framework that redefines how complex systems can sustain ethical coherence, detect and counteract distortion, and cultivate legitimate agency in real time. Building on the philosophical and systemic foundations laid in the preceding chapters, this section translates Tamil Saiva Siddhantam's ontological grammar of Aram (ethical coherence), Aanavam (distortion and entropy), and Adhikaram (agency fitness) into a computable, cybernetic architecture for governance across human, institutional, and artificial systems. You will see how A3 treats ethics not as an external constraint but as a structural property, and how its diagnostic tools from the Six Domains of Distortion to the Adhikaram Pentad enable continuous renewal through recursive loop cycles. By the end of the chapter, you will understand A3 not only as a philosophical synthesis but as a functional design grammar capable of guiding AI governance, organisational transformation, and systemic resilience in the face of accelerating change.*

Introducing the A3 Model – A New Order of Ethical Systemic Intelligence

The preceding sections have traced the contours of our current polycrisis: climate acceleration, AI disruption, institutional erosion, and the entangled feedback loops driving them. These challenges are not separate events but expressions of a deeper systemic incoherence, an inability of our systems to sustain alignment, adapt under pressure, and retain legitimacy at the speed required.

The A3 Model was developed as a direct response to this condition. Its premise is straightforward: no system whether human, institutional, or artificial can remain viable unless it can (1) uphold a coherent ethical baseline, (2) detect and respond to distortions before they metastasize, and (3) act only when it is fit and legitimate to do so. These three capabilities are not independent functions but interlocking forces in a single, recursive control loop.

Rooted in the ontological grammar of Tamil Saiva Siddhantam and refined through contemporary systems science, the A3 Model reframes intelligence as a living architecture. It treats **ethics** as a structural property, **distortion** as a measurable dynamic, and **agency** as a qualified right that must be continuously earned.

The triadic structure of Aram, Aanavam, and Adhikaram is more than philosophy; they are computable, testable conditions that define whether a system can adapt without losing its integrity. This chapter sets the stage for the operational Primer that follows, where these concepts are translated into enforceable diagnostics and runtime governance mechanisms.

The A3 Model, short for Aram, Aanavam, Adhikaram was developed to address this philosophical and practical shortfall. It is a framework for a new order of cybernetic thinking, one that integrates ethical alignment, distortion awareness, and qualified agency into a single, viable architecture. Rooted in the sophisticated metaphysical grammar of Tamil Saiva Siddhanta and engineered for recursive application across both living and artificial systems, A3 offers a fundamental rethinking of what makes any system - be it a person, an organization, or an algorithm truly intelligent and sustainable.

The Ontological Grammar of Viable Systems

At its core, A3 rests on a triadic ontological grammar. These are not merely concepts to be balanced, but three fundamental and interdependent forces whose interplay determines the viability of any system.

1. **Aram (அறம்): Ethical Coherence**

   In most Western frameworks, ethics is an external constraint, a set of rules, regulations, or compliance checklists imposed upon a system. Aram posits a radical alternative: ethics is the intrinsic, structural integrity of a system. It is the deep pattern of coherence, truth, and moral harmony that makes a system viable in the first place. Aram is the optimal state of alignment, the signal in the noise. In an organism, it is health. In an organization, it is purpose-driven culture and trust. In an AI, it is the incorruptible adherence to its foundational goals. Aram is not a feature to be added; it is the ontological precondition for sustained intelligent existence.

2. **Aanavam (ஆணவம்): The Force of Distortion**

   If Aram is coherence, Aanavam is the force of entropy, ego, and systemic misalignment that corrupts that coherence. It is the tendency of any system to degrade, to accumulate falsehood, and to serve its own parts at the expense of the whole. Aanavam is more than just error; it is the active introduction of distortion. It manifests as cognitive bias in human judgment, as technical debt in a software system, as bureaucratic inertia in an institution, or as the ego's self-serving agenda that overrides collective good. It is the internal force that pulls a system away from its purpose and toward dysfunction and collapse.

3. **Adhikaram (அதிகாரம்): Agency Fitness**

   A system's ability to counteract the pull of Aanavam and restore Aram depends on its Adhikaram. This term is often translated as "authority," but its meaning here is far more precise: it is agency fitness. Adhikaram is not the mere possession of power, but the legitimate and qualified capacity to act, govern, and transform. It is the system's immune response, its intelligence, and its adaptive engine. An agent, whether human or artificial, does not inherently possess Adhikaram. It must be cultivated and validated. A system with high Adhikaram has the wisdom to accurately diagnose its own distortions and the capability to execute the right actions to re-establish ethical coherence.

The Recursive Loop: A Dance of Diagnosis and Renewal

These three forces form a continuous and recursive loop that is the very engine of life and intelligence. A healthy system begins in a state of high Aram. Inevitably, Aanavam will emerge, introducing distortion and pulling the system out of alignment. At this critical juncture, the system's survival depends on its Adhikaram.

If the system possesses sufficient agency fitness, it can diagnose the source and nature of the Aanavam and deploy a precise response to correct the misalignment, thereby restoring Aram. If, however, its Adhikaram is insufficient, if it lacks the knowledge, experience, or governance to act effectively, then Aanavam will continue to grow, leading to a death spiral of cascading failures.

This dynamic loop - ***Aram → Aanavam → Adhikaram → Aram*** transforms ethics from a static ideal into a diagnostic, cybernetic process of continuous self-correction.

Beyond Metaphor: A Functional Architecture

The A3 model is not a philosophical metaphor. It is a functioning framework with formal, computable applications. It provides two primary diagnostic tools:

- **The Six Domains of Distortion:** A comprehensive map for diagnosing how, where, and why Aanavam is degrading a system, whether ethically, epistemically, relationally, temporally, contextually, or structurally. For example, climate feedback loops that amplify polar ice melt offer a clear case of reinforcing distortion through ecological feedback mechanisms. This escalating feedback exemplifies Aanavam in triadic recursion: as systemic coherence (Aram) erodes, distortion self-reinforces, necessitating qualified agency (Adhikaram) for restoration. Without this, the cycle repeats and deepens

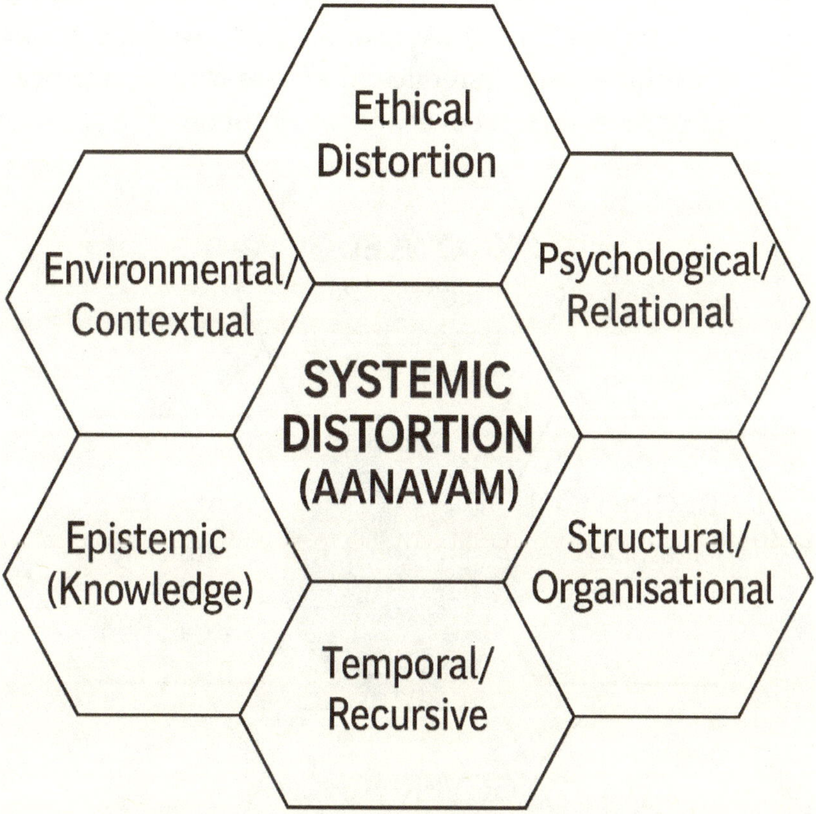

- **The Adhikaram Pentad:** A fivefold model for qualifying agency. It assesses whether an agent is truly fit to act by examining its Knowledge, Right Action, Experience, Governance, and Absorption. A business adapting to a sudden market disruption demonstrates agency fitness: it must draw on contextual knowledge (Knowledge), make timely and effective decisions (Action), leverage prior lessons (Experience), coordinate teams and resources (Governance), and deeply absorb new realities to integrate change (Absorption). A business's adaptive response to market shocks demonstrates the triadic cycle: recognizing misalignment (Aanavam), mobilizing self-qualified agency across the Pentad (Adhikaram), and working toward reestablishing systemic coherence (Aram), a process that must recur at every new disruption.

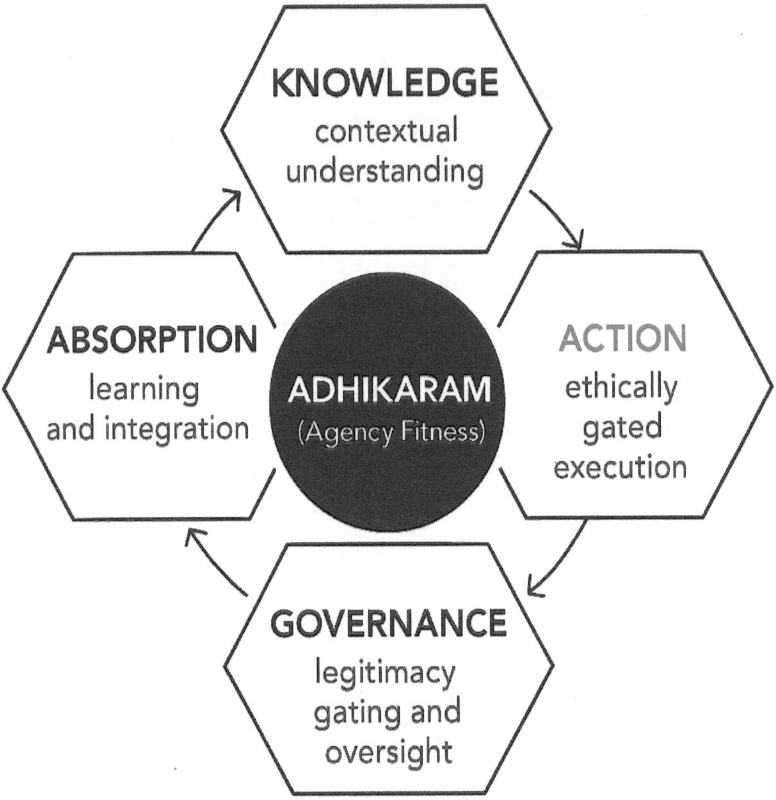

These tools allow us to move beyond abstract discussions and formally assess the health of autonomous systems, diagnose the root causes of organizational dysfunction, and design more resilient public policy. What distinguishes A3 is not only its civilizational depth but its practical universality. It transcends reductionist paradigms by restoring the ethical soul of systems, while exceeding vague holistic frameworks by offering computable, self-iterating diagnostics and clear decision pathways.

In this edition, the A3 model appears not simply as a theoretical concept but as a living architecture - a bridge between ancient metaphysical insight and modern complexity science. It challenges us to engage not only with our systems, but with the fundamental conditions of their viability.

The chapters that follow will serve as both a diagnosis of the modern condition through this lens and a prelude to the A3 Manifesto, where the full architecture and its future-facing implications are unveiled.

Addressing a Common Criticism: Ancient Metaphysics in Modern Tech Contexts

A recurring critique of this work is the integration of ancient Tamil metaphysics, particularly the triadic grammar of Aram, Aanavam, and Adhikaram into contemporary AI and systems governance. This concern often stems from a false dichotomy: that metaphysical insights are inherently pre-scientific or inapplicable to technological domains. However, the A3 Model does not import metaphysics as belief but as epistemic architecture providing a self-iterating logic of ethical coherence, distortion diagnosis, and agency legitimacy. Just as Western systems theory has drawn fruitfully from Greek ontology or Buddhist logic, A3 demonstrates that Tamil Saiva Siddhanta offers an ontologically rich and cybernetically robust foundation for managing complexity, feedback, and ethical drift. Its application to AI governance is neither symbolic nor nostalgic: it is structural, diagnostic, and adaptive.

Chapter-End Reflection Prompts

- Which destabilizing forces resonate most with your own context or sector?

- Can traditional governance models evolve fast enough to manage today's systemic shifts?

- How might ancient civilizational frameworks help design future-fit systems?

APPENDICES A TO D – **THE A3 IMPLEMENTATION TOOLKIT**

Preface

The following appendices translate the A3 Model from its philosophical and systemic foundations (presented in the main chapters) into implementation-ready form for practitioners, policymakers, and system architects.

- **Appendix A - Conceptual Primer to A3**

  Restates the *Aram-Aanavam-Adhikaram* triad for applied use. Identifies core purposes, distinctive features, and structural mechanisms, bridging the conceptual model in the main text to the operational logic in Appendix B. Defines supporting constructs such as the Adhikaram Pentad and the Six Domains of Distortion.

- **Appendix B - Operational Primer: The A3 Model**

  Specifies runtime checks, enforcement logic, and measurable signals for each element of the triad. Describes how the AEVT (A3 Ethical Viability Test), ADRT (A3 Distortion Resolution Tracker), and AFI (A3 Fitness Index) operate at machine tempo to detect ethical drift, surface distortions, gate legitimate agency, and restore systemic coherence.

- **Appendix C - A3 Dynamic Assessment Tool**

  Presents a practical scoring instrument for evaluating ethical systemic intelligence in live systems. Uses the simplified Triadic Synchronisation model to measure cross-domain responsiveness alongside the Systemic Integrity Score (SIS).

Together, these appendices form the technical grammar of A3:

- Appendix A provides the shared conceptual vocabulary.
- Appendix B defines the operational ruleset.
- Appendix C delivers a measurable, repeatable assessment method.

Readers seeking to understand *what A3 is* should begin in the main chapters.

Readers seeking to apply A3 in AI governance, organisational control, or autonomous systems should use these appendices as direct reference material.

APPENDIX A: THE CONCEPTUAL PRIMER TO A3

Aram – Ethical Coherence in the A3 Model

Aram establishes ethical coherence as both an ontological and operational condition: system decisions align with fairness, integrity, and longterm viability; in A3, ethics is not external compliance but the system's governing grammar.

Core Purpose

Ensure that every decision, action, and adaptation maintains ethical legitimacy and contributes to longterm stability for the system and its environment.

Key Mechanisms in A3

- Ethics as Architecture: AEVT enforces ethics in runtime control, not post hoc.
- Contextual Adaptation: Thresholds adapt to context within principled bounds.
- Continuous Validation: Ethical checks run at operational tempo.

Distinctiveness

Unlike compliance ethics (external audits) or constitutional AI (static rule sets), Aram dynamically enforces ethics at machine tempo. Unlike valuesensitive design (frontloaded ethics at design time), Aram sustains value alignment during live operation.

Interplay with the Triad

Aanavam surfaces drift; Adhikaram qualifies action; Aram anchors rightful order.

Adhikaram – The Self-referential Pentad of Agency Fitness (Academic Primer)

Adhikaram formalizes Agency Fitness as a self-adaptive and evolving governance mechanism specified by the pentad: Knowledge, Action, Governance, Experience, Absorption.

- **Knowledge:** Contextual awareness from multisource sensing, epistemic grounding, and interpretive clarity.
- **Action:** Ethically gated execution; actions proceed only when Aram thresholds are met.
- **Governance:** Legitimacy gating via the Agency Fitness Index (AFI); autonomy tiers adjust, or revoke based on realtime system health.
- **Experience:** Outcome capture and validation from live environments to strengthen systemic coherence.
- **Absorption**: Selfevolutionary integration of learning; feedback updates interpretive grammars and capability baselines.

Note on Positioning

For comparative positioning versus VSM and CST, see the main comparative table in your A3 comparison chapter. The pentad treats ethics, distortion, and legitimacy as firstclass control objectives codetermining viability.

Aanavam – Distortion Vigilance in the A3 Model

Aanavam represents systemic distortion, drift, bias, or corruption that undermines coherence, capability, and legitimacy over time. It is measurable, diagnosable, and actionable in complex sociotechnical systems.

Core Purpose

Make distortion visible and actionable so misalignment, capability erosion, or legitimacy loss are surfaced in real time for corrective action.

The Six Domains of Distortion

- **Ethical Distortion:**

  Deviation from core values or principles leading to compromised integrity within the system.

- **Psychological/Relational:**

  Breakdown in interpersonal trust, communication, or relational dynamics affecting collaboration.

- **Structural/Organisational:**

  Faults in the organization's architecture, processes, or governance that disrupt effective functioning.

- **Temporal/Recursive:**

  Failures in timing, adaptation, or synchronous feedback leading to lag or misalignment with changing conditions.

- **Epistemic (Knowledge):**

  Gaps, errors, or distortions in the system's foundational understanding or information base.

- **Environmental/Contextual:**

  Mismatches or disruptions arising from external conditions, surroundings, or broader contextual factors.

Mechanisms in A3 (ADRT – Aanavam Distortion Resolution Tracker)

Continuous Monitoring: Coverage across the six domains.

MultiSignal Detection: Quantitative and qualitative ensembles; avoid singlemetric reliance.

Recursion into Aram and Adhikaram: Aanavam alerts route to Aram checks and Adhikaram gating for immediate governance action.

Governance as Self-evolving Legitimacy (Framing Note)

Governance in A3 is **earned continuously**, not presumed.

- **Aram** anchors value alignment & stakeholder justice.
- **Aanavam** ensures drift is surfaced and routed, not concealed.
- **Adhikaram** gates the **right to act**, adjusting autonomy in real time via AFI.
- Together, they implement a **living constitution** for system behaviour.

Transition

Having explored the philosophical lineage and conceptual primer of A3, the next section shifts from the "why" to the "how," specifying runtime checks and enforcement logic.

APPENDIX B: OPERATIONAL PRIMER: THE A3 MODEL

Core Triad

Conceptual definitions are introduced in Chapter 5 and Appendix A. This appendix specifies runtime checks and enforcement.

Overview

A3's pillars - Aram (ethics), Aanavam (distortion), and Adhikaram (agency) compose a single synchronous control architecture running at operational tempo.

- Aram sets the ethical baseline.
- Aanavam challenges it by surfacing distortions and risks.
- Adhikaram gates the system's right to act, ensuring only fit, legitimate agency proceeds.

Aram – Ethical Coherence (Runtime)

Decisions are legitimate only when they meet enforceable conditions at runtime.

- **Purpose Alignment**
    - **Requirement:** Actions must serve declared mission, scope, and public interest.
    - **Signals:** Purpose consistency ratio; exceptions require justification artefacts.
- **Justice & Stakeholders**
    - **Requirement:** Outcomes equitable across affected groups with fair process and meaningful voice.
    - **Signals:** Disparity deltas; complaint/appeal reversal rates; participation evidence.
- **Proportionality & Harm Limits**
    - **Requirement:** Interventions proportional to risk; minimize harm; abstain/defer when uncertainty is high.
    - **Signals:** Harm proxies; abstention under uncertainty; irreversible action safeguards.
- **Legal/Normative Fit**
    - **Requirement:** Adhere to laws, regulations, and community norms; escalate conflicts preaction.
    - **Signals:** Compliance pass rates; jurisdiction conflicts; escalation latency.
- **Environmental/LongTerm Impact**
    - **Requirement:** Account for sustainability, intergenerational effects, and systemic resilience.
    - **Signals:** Longterm risk index; resource intensity; deferred impact flags.

- **Transparency & Accountability**
    - **Requirement:** Humanreadable reasons; tamper-evident logs; public metrics where appropriate.
    - **Signals:** Explainability coverage; audit completeness; notice delivery.
- **Ethical Override Path**
    - **Requirement:** Clear routes to pause, reverse, or escalate when principles conflict or harms are detected.
    - **Signals:** Override frequency; reason codes; expiry compliance; review outcomes.

Runtime Guard – AEVT

- **Structure:** Rolling pass rates and breach classes (critical/major/minor).
- **Enforcement:** Critical Aram failures gate/suspend flows until thresholds and attestations are restored.
- **Design:** Explicit, risktiered thresholds; pair with appeals and transparency.

Aanavam – Distortion Awareness (Runtime)

Domains are defined in Appendix A; runtime focuses on signals and enforcement.

Signals (Illustrative Ensembles)

- **Epistemic:** PSI/JS/KL shifts, OOD scores, calibration drift, missingness patterns.
- **Structural/Organisational:** Escalation loop frequency, queue skews, approval asymmetry, churn markers.

- **Psychological/Relational:** Reviewer disagreement spikes, adversarial prompts, refusal/hallucination proxies, sentiment drift.
- **Temporal/Recursive:** Error motif recurrence, lagadjusted performance shifts, reappearing issues.
- **Environmental/Contextual:** Feature drift, policy version flips, capacity/latency anomalies, geographic cohort shifts.
- **Ethical Distortion:** Aram-Aanavam inconsistencies, rising appeals amidst "green" metrics, whistleblower flags.

Runtime Guard – ADRT

- **Structure:** Multisignal ensemble assigns severity α (local/input), β (behavioural/process), γ (governance/output).
- **Enforcement:**
    - α: Constrain affected path; enable guardrails; increase human sampling.
    - β: Cap autonomy; ratelimit/freeze deploys; trigger triage.
    - γ: Suspend/rollback flow; declare incident; require recalibration before reentry.
- **Design:** Multisignal confirmation + hysteresis; explain what distorted, where, and why.

Adhikaram – Legitimate Agency (Runtime)

Pentad definitions are in Appendix A; runtime specifies metrics and gating.

- **Knowledge Measures:** Task accuracy; calibration; context adherence; uncertainty estimation quality.

- **Action Measures:** Safe tool invocation; reversiblefirst behaviour; autonomy cap adherence; rollback success.
- **Experience Measures:** Learning retention; recurrence rate of resolved failures; improvement velocity.
- **Absorption Measures:** Change adoption latency; MTTR for ethics/drift breaches; stability during recalibration.
- **Governance Measures:** Override hygiene (twoperson rule adherence); audit completeness; authority transition justification.

Runtime Guard – AFI

- **Structure:** AFI aggregates capacities, riskweighted by task criticality, blast radius, and uncertainty; produces autonomytier cap.
- **Enforcement:** Autonomy levels (e.g., L0-L4/L5) capped by AFI; highrisk tools require high AFI and clean Aram/Aanavam; midrun AFI drops autodowngrade autonomy and revoke highrisk tools.
- **Design:** AFI is auditable; monotonicity prevents high autonomy with weak critical capacities.

The Recursive Loop – Diagnosis, Correction, Renewal (Enforcement Mapping)

A narrative of the loop appears in Chapter 5; enforcement mapping is below.

- **Step 1: Aram sets the ethical baseline (AEVT)**

  Define thresholds and critical classes; critical failures are legitimacy failures; operations are constrained or suspended by rule.

- **Step 2: Aanavam detects and localizes distortion (ADRT)**

  Classify α/β/γ; cap autonomy, ratelimit, or suspend; minimize time under illegitimate operation.

- **Step 3: Adhikaram gates agency and orchestrates reentry (AFI)**

  Grant/downgrade/withdraw authority based on AFI; reentry requires restored Aram, acceptable Aanavam severity, and AFI in band; safetycritical reentry may require human cosign.

- **Continuous Renewal**

  Experience/Absorption embed lessons; Governance reviews overrides to prevent normalization of deviance.

Operational Implications

- Machinetempo adjudication reduces governance latency from hours/days to cycles/seconds.
- Authority becomes a computable state that shifts with ethical and distortion signals.
- Systems default to safe abstention or constrained operation under uncertainty and reenter with documented recalibration.

Implementation Notes

- **Thresholding and Risk Tiers**: Define perdomain thresholds for AEVT, ADRT, AFI; stricter thresholds and human cosigns for safetycritical flows.
- **Evidence and Attestation**: Log all guard triggers and actions with signed, contentaddressed bundles; maintain privacypreserving public summaries.

- **Overrides and Appeals:** Overrides lift constraints temporarily; never bypass hard suspensions from critical ethical failures or γclass distortions; provide accessible appeal paths; track reversal rates.
- **Transparency by Design:** Display concise notices when constraints/suspensions occur, including reasons and next steps; publish periodic AEVT/ADRT/AFI dashboards, incidents, and remediation.
- **Calibration and Stability:** Pair univariate drift tests with complementary checks and outcome disparities; add hysteresis and multisignal confirmation to reduce false trips and flapping.

Anti-Gaming & Goodhart Safeguards

- **Multi-signal confirmation** (never rely on a single metric to pass/fail).
- **Hysteresis** windows to prevent flapping around thresholds.
- **Metric rotation & canaries** to deter metric tunnelling.
- **Alert suppression audit**: log and review suppressed ADRT alerts.
- **Counterfactual probes**: periodic "red-team" injections to assess guard integrity.
- **Penalties for bypass**: governance violations degrade AFI and trigger audits.

Human-in-the-Loop Governance (RACI)

Decision	R	A	C	I
Suspend flow (γ distortion / critical Aram fail)	Ethics Lead	System Owner	Security/Privacy, Domain SME	Independent Auditor, Ops
Autonomy downgrade	Ethics Lead	System Owner	Domain SME	Auditor, Ops
Re-entry after fix	Ethics Lead	System Owner	Auditor, Domain SME	Ops, Product
Override (time-limited)	Domain SME + Ethics Lead	System Owner	Security/Privacy	Auditor, Ops
Appeal decision	Independent Reviewer	Ethics Lead	System Owner	Complainant, Ops
Incident closure	Ethics Lead	System Owner	Auditor	All stakeholders

Quick Reference: Roles of the Triad

- Aram answers "Should this be done?" with enforceable ethical conditions.
- Aanavam answers "What is distorting coherence?" with localized, severitygraded detection.
- Adhikaram answers "Is the system fit to act now?" with authority gating and controlled reentry.

Together, they form a living constitution for system behaviour: ethics sets the law, distortion enforces vigilance, and agency earns the right to act again and again, at the speed of operation.

APPENDIX C: THE A3 DYNAMIC ASSESSMENT TOOL: A FRAMEWORK FOR ETHICAL SYSTEMIC INTELLIGENCE

Foreword

In an era shaped by autonomous and complex systems, the imperative to embed ethics, accountability, and adaptive capacity is paramount. Traditional ethical frameworks designed for human decisionmaking often fall short when applied to selfgoverning algorithms and intricate sociotechnical ecologies. This book introduces the A3 Dynamic Assessment Tool, a pioneering framework developed to address this gap. Drawing from ancient philosophical wisdom and modern cybernetic principles, the A3 model provides a holistic lens to evaluate, guide, and enhance the systemic integrity of complex autonomous entities. It invites a shift from reactive ethics to a proactive, recursive, and integrated approach to building systems that are not only powerful, but inherently good.

1. Introduction to the A3 Framework for Ethical Systems

The relentless advance of artificial intelligence and autonomous systems demands a commensurate evolution in how their ethical dimensions are conceived, designed, and governed. Simply programming rules or relying on external oversight is insufficient for systems that learn, adapt, and operate in dynamic, unpredictable environments. The A3 framework emerges as a novel cybernetic architecture, positing that genuine ethical intelligence is an intrinsic property arising from the continuous, recursive interplay of three ontological forces: Aram, Aanavam, and Adhikaram.

More than a linear checklist, A3 offers a dynamic, selfcorrecting paradigm: for any system to achieve true autonomy and foster wellbeing, it must sustain a perpetual dialogue between its inherent purpose, its inevitable distortions, and its capacity for legitimate action. The A3 Dynamic Assessment Tool operationalizes these concepts, providing a practical method for evaluating and developing ethical systemic intelligence, a compass for navigating 21stcentury ethical landscapes toward systems that are not only intelligent, but wise, resilient, and aligned with human flourishing.

2. The Core Elements of A3

The A3 framework is a recursive triad in which each element continuously informs and influences the others.

2.1 Aram (அறம்): Ethical Coherence and Integrity

Aram signifies foundational alignment with ethical purpose, values, and the moral, legal, and environmental norms of the operating context; it represents the inherent "rightness" of a system's being and action.

Key characteristics of strong Aram:

- **Clarity of Purpose:** A clearly defined and communicated ethical mission guiding all operations.

- **Value Alignment:** Actions and outcomes consistently reflect stated moral commitments.
- **Normative Embedding**: Environmental, legal, and societal norms are deeply integrated into processes and decision logic.
- **Resource Stewardship:** Time, energy, and computational resources reinforce declared values.
- **Process-Outcome Harmony:** Methods are as ethically sound as results.
- **LongTerm Accountability:** Future consequences are accounted for to ensure sustainability.
- **Resilience in Stress:** Ethical values remain steadfast under adaptation, crisis, or high stress.
- **Stakeholder Perception:** Stakeholders perceive alignment between values and behaviour, fostering trust.
- **Transparency:** Decision logic is clear, comprehensible, and open to appropriate scrutiny.
- **ValueReinforcement Feedback:** Iterative feedback loops continuously reinforce ethical values.

2.2 Aanavam (ஆணவம்): Systemic Distortion and Entropy

Aanavam is internal veiling or systemic distortion ("egoic drift"): the tendency toward misalignment, fragmentation, or departure from ethical coherence. It is inherent, not merely a "bug," and when recognized becomes a vital signal for adaptation.

Indicators of Aanavam:

- **Communication Breakdowns:** Recurring failures in mutual understanding or information exchange.

- **Role-Expectation Misalignment:** Discrepancies between roles and expected contributions/outcomes.
- **Ecological Contradiction:** Operations harming the broader environment or contradicting stated goals.
- **Misaligned Motivations:** Incentives contributing to ethical drift or incoherence.
- **Role Confusion/Lack of Purpose:** Persistent ambiguity about functions in larger context.
- **Disconnection/Fragmentation:** Siloed operations or broken interfaces across relationships.
- **Externalization of Impacts:** Overlooking or offloading negative socioenvironmental consequences.
- **Information-Relevance Gap:** Disconnect between information and its ethical significance/actionability.
- **Resistance to Feedback:** Leadership/components resisting adaptive critique or feedback.
- **Governance-Pressure Misalignment:** Tension between internal ethical governance and external pressures.

2.3 Adhikaram (அதிகாரம்): Legitimate Adaptive Agency

Adhikaram represents rightful capacity to act, adapt, and govern reflexively; agency that is ethically informed, contextually appropriate, and continuously revisable through learning and recalibration.

Hallmarks of strong Adhikaram:

- **Active Learning:** Systematically learning from outcomes and integrating feedback.
- **Responsive DecisionMaking:** Agile responses to detected ethical misalignments.

- **BuiltIn Reflexivity:** Embedded mechanisms for self-reflection and sensemaking.
- **Actionable Knowledge:** Capability to translate insights into implementable knowledge.
- **Intentional Closure:** Clear feedback loops across action, experience, and adaptation.
- **Stakeholder Engagement:** Inclusive shaping of adaptive responses.
- **Support for MicroAgency:** Enabling bottomup innovation and decentralized problemsolving.
- **Distributed Governance:** Structures to resolve ethical tension across layers/components.
- **Scenario Modelling:** Proactive modelling to anticipate ethical risks.
- **Adaptive Scaling:** Governance that scales with complexity while maintaining coherence.

2.4 Triadic Synchronization: The Dynamic Balance

Triadic Synchronization represents the dynamic interplay among Aram, Aanavam, and Adhikaram the continuous loop wherein detection of Aanavam prompts Adhikaram to restore Aram.

Indicators of strong Triadic Synchronization:

- **Interconnected Tracking**: Coherence, distortion, and agency are monitored in relation.
- **CrossDomain Responsiveness:** Misalignment in one domain triggers timely, proportionate responses in the others.

- **Proactive Coherence Restoration:** Reflexive governance restores coherence before failure cascades.
- **Structured Feedback Loops:** Formal interfaces for triadic feedback.
- **Dynamic Balance Maintenance:** A consistent equilibrium among values, distortions, and transformative actions.

3. The A3 Dynamic Assessment Tool: Assessment Sheets

Rate each item from 1 to 5 based on observed evidence.

Section 1: Aram (Ethical Coherence Index – ECI)

Assesses clarity in ethical purpose and alignment with moral and operational commitments.

Item list (score each 1–5; include weighted score if applicable):

Section 1 – Aram (Ethical Coherence Index)

	Assessment Item	Score	Weighted
1	Clarity in ethical purpose and function		
2	Actions align with stated ethical commitments		
3	Environmental/legal/moral norms embedded		
4	Resources used in ways reflecting values		
5	Right process for right outcome		
6	Long-term consequences aligned with purpose		
7	Values maintained during stress/adaptation		
8	Stakeholders perceive value-action alignment		
9	Transparent decision-making logic		
10	Feedback loops aligned to value reinforcement		
Total (ECI): _____			

Section 2: Aanavam (Systemic Distortion Index – DIS)

Identifies recurring misalignment patterns indicating departure from ethical coherence.

Item list:

	Assessment Item	Score	Weighted
1	Recurring breakdowns in communication		
2	Role-expectation misalignment		
3	Ecological contradiction or overreach		
4	Misaligned motivations causing ethical drift		
5	Persistent role confusion		
6	Relationship/interface fragmentation		
7	Socio-environmental impacts externalised		
8	Gap between info flows and ethical relevance		
9	Leadership resists adaptive feedback		
10	Internal vs external value misalignment		
Total (DIS): ____			

Section 3: Adhikaram (Adaptive Agency Index – AAI)

Assesses capacity for legitimate, adaptive action and reflexive governance.

Item list:

	Assessment Item	**Score**	**Weighted**
1	System learns from feedback		
2	Decisions address ethical misalignment		
3	Reflexivity built into governance		
4	Generates actionable knowledge		
5	Closure between action, experience & adaptation		
6	Stakeholders engaged in shaping responses		
7	Support for bottom-up innovation		
8	Distributed governance for ethical resolution		
9	Scenarios model future ethical risks		
10	Governance scales across complexity		
Total (AAI): _____			

Section 4: Triadic Synchronization

Evaluates dynamic balance across Aram, Aanavam, and Adhikaram.

Item list:

1. Coherence, distortion, and agency tracked in relation.
2. Misalignment in one domain triggers responses in others.
3. Proactive restoration of coherence via reflexive governance.
4. Structured interfaces for triadic feedback loops.
5. Maintenance of dynamic balance among value, misalignment, and transformation.

4. Scoring Guide and Interpretation

Use simple weighting initially (Weighted Score = Score × 1), with the option to assign higher weights to critical items in advanced applications.

Calculations

- Total Aram (ECI): Sum of Section 1 weighted scores.
- Total Aanavam (DIS): Sum of Section 2 weighted scores.
- Total Adhikaram (AAI): Sum of Section 3 weighted scores.

Systemic Integrity Score (SIS)

SIS = ECI − DIS + AAI

Interpretation

- Higher ECI: Strong ethical foundations and clarity of purpose; values are welldefined and consistently reflected.
- Lower DIS: Fewer active distortions/misalignments; reduced "egoic drift."
- Higher AAI: Robust adaptive capabilities and legitimate, responsive action.
- High SIS: Ethically coherent, minimally distorted, and strongly adaptive, indicating trustworthy systemic integrity and capacity for selfgovernance.
- Low or Negative SIS: Significant ethical challenges, high distortion, or insufficient adaptive agency prioritizing urgent intervention and redesign.

The Crucial Role of Triadic Synchronization (TS)

SIS is an aggregate measure; TS reveals dynamic resilience.

Why TS matters:

- **Beyond Static Measures:** High SIS can mask weak coupling among domains.
- **RealTime Responsiveness:** Indicates whether detected distortion (Aanavam) triggers timely, proportionate agency (Adhikaram) to restore coherence (Aram).
- **Latent Fragility Detection:** Low TS allows isolated distortions to escalate, cause disproportionate damage, and create instability not visible in static scores.

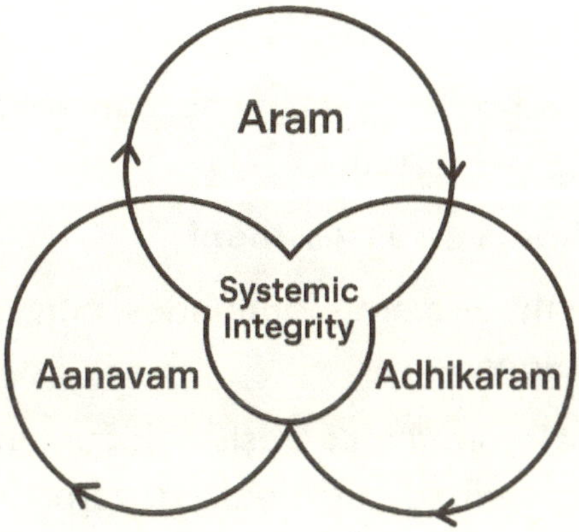

Analogy

A highperformance vehicle may have excellent components (engine, steering, brakes), yielding a strong aggregate score; but if the control systems do not coordinate during an unexpected skid (distortion), the car fails in practice. Likewise, low TS signals critical vulnerability in selfgovernance under dynamic conditions even when ECI and AAI are high.

5. Applying the A3 Dynamic Assessment Tool

This tool is for continuous improvement and ethical system design.

Who should use this tool?

- AI Developers and Engineers: Embed ethics from design through deployment.
- AI Ethicists and Researchers: Analyse and refine ethical governance of autonomous agents.
- Organizational Leaders: Assess sociotechnical systemic integrity.

- Policymakers and Regulators: Develop robust frameworks for responsible AI.
- Any Stakeholder: Seeking accountable, resilient, ethically aligned systems.

How to conduct an assessment

1. Define the System: Boundaries, purpose, and primary functions.
2. Gather Information: Design documents, logs, stakeholder feedback, incidents, governance structures.
3. Score Each Item: Rate 1-5 with evidencebased justifications.
4. Calculate Domain Scores: ECI, DIS, AAI, and Triadic Synchronization.
5. Calculate SIS: SIS = ECI – DIS + AAI.
6. Interpret and Analyse: Examine domain scores and, critically, TS for coupling quality.
7. Develop Actionable Insights: Improve Aram, reduce Aanavam, enhance Adhikaram, strengthen TS.
8. Iterate and reassess: Implement changes, monitor impact, and reassess to track progress.

Commitment

This tool embodies a commitment to recursive legitimacy shifting from static ethics to dynamic, continuously evolving ethical intelligence.

Conclusion – The Path to True Autonomy

The A3 Dynamic Assessment Tool offers a pathway to autonomous systems that are capable, ethical, and trustworthy. By assessing Aram, Aanavam, and Adhikaram and, crucially, their Triadic Synchronization, it becomes possible to understand true systemic integrity and the capacity for legitimate selfgovernance. This framework is a call to embed accountability into system fabric so that ethical resilience is an emergent property of continuous selfcorrection. As autonomy advances, tools like A3 will be indispensable to ensure that the intelligence created serves humanity's highest values, enabling human-machine coevolution with coherence and trust.

APPENDIX D: IMPLEMENTATION AND PILOT PATHWAY

This appendix provides a structured, step-by-step pathway for piloting the A3 Model in a real-world operational environment. It offers performance metrics (the "A3 Delta"), a minimal technical deployment stack, integrated governance safeguards, and a recommended pilot approach. The objective is to enable rapid, low-risk implementation while delivering measurable evidence of A3's impact on system responsiveness, legitimacy, fairness, and stability.

1. A3 Delta: What to Instrument

A3 Delta defines a suite of metrics tracking improvements in system performance under A3 governance, as compared with a pre-A3 baseline. This consistent evaluation framework focuses on responsiveness, ethical legitimacy, fairness, and operational stability.

Metric	Target	Measurement	Example
Governance Latency	<1 second (high-risk)	Real-time event logs	How quickly a delivery robot halts on path deviation
Time-Under-Illegitimate-Operation	<5 minutes	Audit logs, ethical rule violations	Time discriminatory ads run before intervention
Utility Retention	≥95% of baseline output	Error rates, throughput, satisfaction	Maintaining delivery schedules post-A3 intervention
Equity Deltas	≥10% parity improvement	Statistical audits, user feedback	Reduced mis-ID gaps in facial recognition
Override Quality	<10% reversal rate	Structured review by independent auditors	Moderator judgment matches for flagged posts
Recovery Quality	<5% deviation from expected	Post-intervention performance analysis	Algorithm avoids repeat errors over 7 days
Trust Signals	NPS >50, <2% complaints	Surveys, appeals, NPS tracking	Low complaints in healthcare AI oversight

Note: PSI (Population Stability Index), KL divergence (Kullback-Leibler), and OOD (Out-of-Distribution) detection are key methods used in fair and stable system monitoring.

Implementation Steps:

- Weeks 1–2: Define baselines using historical data and direct stakeholder input.
- Assign data scientists for protocol design, auditors for validation.
- Mitigate incomplete baselines with small-scale pilots and transparent reporting.

2. Minimal Reference Stack (Weeks 1–4 Build)

A deployable four-week stack integrates all core A3 components for governance and oversight:

- **Policy-as-Code (AEVT):** Encodes ethical rules into enforceable policies via purpose tags, risk tiers, and harm caps.
- *Example: Caps discriminatory outcomes in hiring algorithms at 3%.*
- *Implementation: YAML-based rules (Week 2 testing).*
- **Distortion Engine (ADRT):** Detects distortions (Aanavam) using PSI, KL divergence, and OOD monitoring, classifying severity as α (local), β (process-wide), γ (systemic governance failure).
- Implementation: Machine learning monitors, sensitivity calibration (Week 3).
- **Agency Gate (AFI):** Calculates a weighted Adhikaram score over ethics, stability, risk, performance, and trust, assigning autonomy levels (L0–L4).
- Implementation: Weighted scoring model, assessed Week 3.
- **Runtime Controller:** Executes A3 actions (suspen-

sions, autonomy downgrades, re-admissions) using API triggers and failover protocols.

- *Implementation: API integration, failover tests (Week 4).*
- **Explainer & Logs:** Delivers human-readable justifications and secure, append-only audit bundles.
- *Implementation: Template summaries, audit logs (Week 4).*

Team Requirements:

- 3-5 engineers
- 2 data scientists
- 1 ethicist
- Cloud infrastructure supporting real-time processing

3. Governance Safeguards & Ethics

Robust guardrails are embedded to ensure minimal harm and maintain system trust:

- Safer Defaults: For ADRT confidence levels below 80%, the system constrains actions or abstains. Overrides require two reviewers within 24 hours, with exceptions auto-expiring in 48 hours.
- Privacy: Personal Identifiable Information (PII) is removed via tokenisation; only cryptographic proofs are stored, not raw data.
- Appeals: Stakeholders can challenge A3 decisions. Resolution targets are under 72 hours, with outcomes feeding continuous ADRT refinement.

Implementation Notes:

- Engage ethicists and legal teams early (Week 1).

- Prioritise high-impact cases for triage, automating where possible to avoid overload.

4. Pilot Pathway (Weeks 5-8)

- Weeks 1-2: Define A3 Delta metrics, AEVT policies, and baseline measures; select a low-stakes pilot domain to minimise risk.
- Weeks 3-4: Build and validate AEVT, ADRT, AFI, and runtime controller; simulate common distortions; apply governance guardrails.
- Weeks 5-6: Integrate all modules, conduct end-to-end testing, and gather stakeholder feedback.
- Weeks 7-8: Launch the pilot, monitor performance in real time, refine based on trust signals, and prepare a detailed pilot report.

Risk Mitigation:

- Conduct pre-pilot workshops to build participant trust.
- Use phased testing to detect integration errors early.
- Maintain manual override contingency plans for critical failures.

A3 Pilot Pathway Summary (Weeks 1-8)

Phase	Activities	Risk Mitigation Measures
Weeks 1-2	Define A3 Delta metrics and baseline; set ethical policies; identify pilot environment	- Pre-pilot workshops for stakeholder trust
Weeks 3-4	Build and test AEVT, ADRT, AFI, runtime controller; simulate distortions; implement guardrails	- Phased testing to catch integration bugs early
Weeks 5-6	Integrate modules; conduct end-to-end testing; gather feedback	- Manual override protocols for critical failures
Weeks 7-8	Launch pilot; monitor metrics in real time; refine system and report results	- Continuous monitoring and feedback loops

Notes:

- Risk mitigation measures are threaded throughout all phases, not just isolated steps.
- Each phase is designed to ensure both operational reliability and stakeholder confidence, with contingency protocols in place from start to finish.

Outcome

This pathway enables A3 to be deployed with provable improvements in ethical and operational performance, minimising disruption and enhancing stakeholder confidence. The result is a resilient, adaptive governance layer applicable across diverse environments and regulatory requirements. Its modular architecture allows seamless adaptation across sectors and regulatory regimes, making A3 a scalable foundation for responsible AI.

APPENDIX E: SIMULATING RECURSIVE ETHICAL GOVERNANCE

A Case Study of the A3 Model in Municipal AI Decision-Making

This appendix presents a simulated case study demonstrating the practical application of the A3 Model in municipal AI governance. It illustrates how recursive ethical realignment can address systemic distortion within an AI-driven housing allocation system, restoring ethical coherence, legitimacy, and public trust. The case merges both structured simulation stages and a narrative account of human and civic impact, providing a publication-ready model for illustrating A3 in action.

Case Scenario: AI-Driven Housing Allocation System

A mid-sized city, aiming for efficiency and fairness, deploys an AI-driven system to automate public housing allocation. The system's criteria - urgency, income, and family size were designed for objectivity.

However, within weeks, community backlash arises. Citizens report receiving coded rejection notices such as *"Ineligible - Code 404"* without explanation or appeal. A local newspaper highlights the case of a single mother of three from a minority community, who was abruptly denied housing support. Civil society groups amplify concerns of bias, opacity, and accountability failure.

This triggering event activates the city's A3 Governance Framework, initiating adaptive ethical diagnostics and re-alignment.

This diagram captures the iterative nature of A3, escalating from distortion detection to suspension, realignment, and recursive reboot.

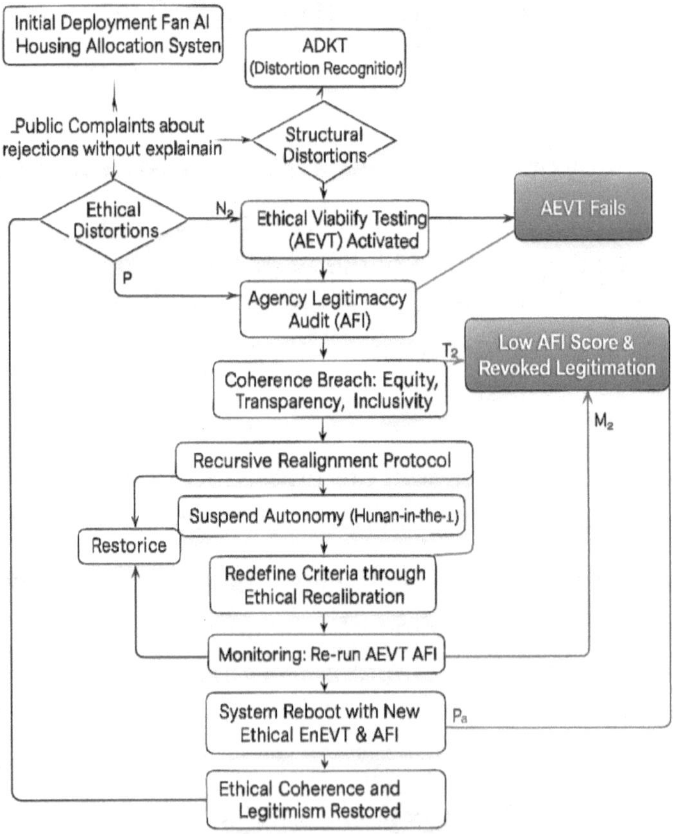

Simulation Framework

Stage 1: Initial Trigger

- **Trigger:** Rejection codes ("Ineligible - 404") provoke public outrage.
- **Response:** A3's Aanavam Distortion Recognition Tracker (ADRT) activated to assess systemic drift.

Stage 2: Distortion Detection (ADRT)

- **Input Sources:** AI decision logs, citizen complaints, media reports, and policy statements.
- **Findings:**
- **Structural Distortion:** High → No appeal or override mechanisms.
- **Ethical Distortion:** Medium-High → Disproportionate rejections for minority applicants.
- **Say-Do Gap:** Public messaging on equity contradicted by actual system outcomes.

Conclusion: Early evidence of systemic drift, prioritizing speed and efficiency over equity and accountability.

Stage 3: Ethical Viability Testing (AEVT)

- **Framework:** City's Digital Ethics Charter.
- **Results:**
- **Failed:** Equity, Transparency, Due Process, Inclusivity.
- **Passed:** Efficiency, Availability.

Conclusion: Ethical coherence breach confirmed.

Stage 4: Agency Legitimacy Audit (AFI)

- **Audit Dimensions:** knowledge coherence, escalation handling, governance responsiveness, absorptive capacity.

- **Score:** 0.38 / 1.0 (below 0.6 threshold).

Conclusion: AI system revoked of legitimacy to act autonomously.

Stage 5: Recursive Realignment and Reboot

- **Protocol Activated:**
    - Autonomous decisions suspended.
    - Human-in-the-Loop fallback enforced.
    - Public alert issued via ethics dashboard.
- **Stakeholder Panel Convened:** Ethicists, technologists, civil society groups, community representatives, and affected citizens.
- **Redesign Focus:**
    - Redefining "urgency" using community narratives.
    - Implementing equity-weighted scoring.
    - Introducing explainability and appeals process.

Stage 6: Post-Reboot Monitoring

- **AEVT Results:** 5 of 6 categories passed (transparency and due process restored).
- **AFI Score:** 0.72 (fitness to act autonomously re-established).
- **Public Trust:** Confidence surveys +35%.
- **Bias Indicators:** Reduced by over 60%.

Case Outcomes

This simulation demonstrates how the A3 Model operates not just as oversight, but as a reflexive governance framework:

- Distortion is proactively diagnosed (ADRT).

- Ethical coherence is stress-tested (AEVT).
- Agency legitimacy is audited (AFI).
- Autonomous action is withdrawn and restored based on recursive legitimacy, closing the loop between system design, governance standards, and lived public values.

Reflections

The case illustrates how A3 treats systemic distortion not as a software bug, but as an early governance signal. Instead of remaining reactive, governance becomes recursive suspending, recalibrating, and rebooting systems in alignment with declared values and public trust.

Future Work

The scenario presented required external governance intervention (e.g., human-in-the-loop fallback, ethics panel). A more mature A3 architecture would include a built-in ontological reboot layer (e.g., Shunyam protocol), enabling the AI system to:

1. Autonomously suspend itself upon detecting an ethical breach.
2. Reconfigure its interpretive grammar to restore alignment with governance fundamentals.
3. Only resume service once ethical coherence, agency legitimacy, and ontological integrity are internally re-established.

This represents A3's vision of true autonomy: the system not as unchecked automation, but as a self-governing, ethically reflexive entity capable of self-withdrawal, self-reboot, and self-legitimation.

Case Summary

- Tools Applied: ADRT (distortion tracking), AEVT (ethical viability), AFI (legitimacy audit).
- Problem: Ethical drift in AI housing allocation (opacity, inequity, loss of legitimacy).
- Intervention: Recursive suspension, ethical redesign, stakeholder participation.
- Outcome: Ethical coherence and legitimacy restored; public trust rebuilt.
- Contribution: Demonstrates A3's recursive governance as an operational model for municipal AI ethics.

Keywords: A3 Model, ADRT, AEVT, AFI, recursive governance, AI ethics, housing allocation, systemic distortion, ethical recursion, Shunyam protocol.

Triadic Case Vignettes for A3 Loop

These practical (hypothetical) vignettes demonstrate A3's recursive loop in action across AI, climate systems, and global supply chains. You will see how systemic misalignments are diagnosed and corrected using the model's formal architecture.

1. Healthcare AI: Diagnosing Bias in Predictive Risk Models

- **Aram:** An AI system is used to prioritize patients for preventative cardiovascular care. Originally trained with population health data, its goal is to equitably allocate clinical attention to those at highest risk.
- **Aanavam:** Over time, the system begins underdiagnosing risk in ethnic minority groups due to underrepresentation in training data. The distortion remains undetected as systemic output metrics (e.g. hospital throughput) appear to improve.
- **Adhikaram:** Upon independent audit, a triadic diagnostic using AEVT reveals *epistemic distortion* and *structural misalignment*. The agency fitness pentad is triggered - clinical teams revise data pipelines (Knowledge), retrain models (Action), apply lessons from past bias cases (Experience), update institutional oversight policies (Governance), and absorb the lived narratives of underserved communities (Absorption). Aram is progressively restored.

•

Healthcare AI – Takeaways

Key Insight: Even well-intentioned AI systems can deepen inequality through unnoticed systemic bias.

A3 in Action: The AEVT diagnostic and Adhikaram pentad allow for multi-layered, ethical recalibration.

Lesson: Aram cannot be presumed from output success; legitimacy must be continually re-established through recursive metrics.

A3 - Benefits

- Ethical AI governance requires recursively adaptive diagnostics, not just fairness at training time.
- Bias is often systemically latent, emerging only under stress or drift.
- The A3 loop helps realign structural, epistemic, and institutional coherence.

2. Climate Modelling: Feedback Loops in Arctic Ice Melt

- **Aram:** A climate feedback model predicts long-term ice shelf stability based on global emission scenarios. Multinational agencies coordinate emissions caps using this predictive clarity.
- **Aanavam:** Subsurface methane release and ocean current anomalies introduce nonlinear accelerations not captured in the original model. Political inertia and bureaucratic silos prevent rapid response. The system underestimates danger and *temporal* and *relational distortion* grows.
- **Adhikaram:** A multi-scale recursive system governance body, guided by A3 principles, initiates layered diagnostics. Scientists update boundary conditions

(Knowledge), realign carbon pricing policies (Action), apply insights from glacier collapse precedents (Experience), restructure inter-agency cooperation (Governance), and integrate Indigenous ecological forecasting (Absorption). A deeper Aram emerges.

Climate Modelling - Takeaways

Key Insight: Static models fail under dynamic, nonlinear environmental acceleration.

A3 in Action: The recursive architecture enables feedback updates beyond political bottlenecks.

Lesson: Distortion can emerge from epistemic delay; systemic coherence depends on anticipatory governance and inclusion.

A3 - Benefits

- Nonlinearity and lag in climate feedback require recursive recalibration, not fixed baselines.
- A3's recursive grammar supports multi-scalar coordination and correction.
- Epistemic humility is key: Indigenous knowledge and historic precedents enhance legitimacy.

3. Global Supply Chains: Semiconductor Crisis

- **Aram:** Global just-in-time semiconductor logistics operate efficiently with balanced flows across Taiwan, South Korea, and U.S. assembly networks.
- **Aanavam:** A combination of geopolitical tension, pandemic-related shutdowns, and sudden demand spikes cause cascading disruptions. Supply models fail to update. Corporations begin hoarding. Nation-

alistic protectionism increases *contextual,* and *governance distortions* intensify.

- **Adhikaram:** A3-loop diagnostics are applied at an intergovernmental level. Stakeholders co-develop resilient models (Knowledge), implement modular inventory frameworks (Action), draw on 2011 Fukushima disruption patterns (Experience), establish international cooperative pacts (Governance), and reflect on fragilities in the global dependency structure (Absorption). Systemic coherence is partially re-established.

Semiconductor Supply Chains – Takeaways

Key Insight: Fragile global dependencies collapse quickly when unforeseen stressors cascade.

A3 in Action: Multilateral A3 diagnostics foster adaptive frameworks and legitimacy realignment.

Lesson: Robustness demands not only logistics but recursive legitimacy and ethical redundancy.

A3 - Benefits

- JIT models lack adaptive ethical intelligence under systemic shock.
- A3 enables resilient governance and global coordination through ethical recursion.
- True robustness arises from absorption, not efficiency alone.

Summary: Case Vignettes

These three cases illustrate how A3's triadic loop of Aram → Aanavam → Adhikaram operates across domains:

- Healthcare AI demonstrates ethical bias detection and correction.
- Climate modelling showcases recursion in planetary-scale system adaptation.
- Supply chains show governance resilience through ethical absorption. The A3 model is universally applicable, dynamically recursive, and ethically grounded for governing complexity.

These vignettes illustrate the recursive loop of Aram (see Glossary) → Aanavam (see Glossary,) → Adhikaram (see Glossary,) in distinct real-world contexts, demonstrating the universality and practical diagnostic power of the A3 Model.

Practical Implementation: How A3 Is Applied

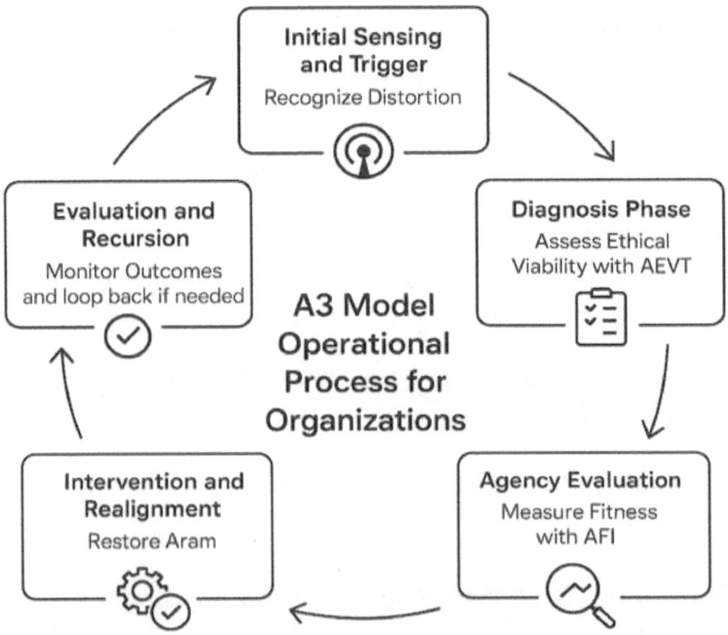

Key Practical Features:

- Recursive Diagnosis: The A3 Model enables the continuous detection of systemic drift or distortion (Aanavam), not just through technical errors but via ethical and legitimacy criteria.
- Metrics and Tools: Tools like the AEVT (Ethical Viability Test), ADRT (Distortion Resolution Tracker), and AFI (Agency Fitness Index) allow organizations to formally assess alignment, distortion, and qualified agency within their AI systems, policies, or organizational practices.
- Organizational Transformation: Organizations are encouraged to move from static compliance to dynamic ethical recursion, learning to sense, diagnose, and realign not just technical processes, but mission, authority, and stakeholder legitimacy.

Challenges and Areas for Further Refinement

While the A3 Model offers a robust framework for addressing systemic complexity through ethical recursion, no model is without its hurdles. This section explores key challenges that may arise in its application, drawing from the polycrisis diagnosis and the model's triadic structure. These are not insurmountable barriers but opportunities for refinement, either in future editions of this work or in the forthcoming A3 Manifesto. By acknowledging them, we underscore the model's commitment to self-reflection and adaptive evolution mirroring the recursive principles it advocates.

Resistance to Ethical Recursion

Deeply entrenched organizational cultures or powerful vested interests may resist the continuous self-assessment and realignment demanded by A3's recursive ethical framework. For instance, in hierarchical institutions where authority is centralized, the model's emphasis on detecting Aanavam (systemic distortion) and cultivating Adhikaram (agency fitness) could be perceived as a threat to established power dynamics. Leaders accustomed to top-down control might view the ongoing ethical diagnostics such as AEVT or ADRT as disruptive or unnecessary, leading to superficial adoption rather than genuine integration. This resistance could manifest as "ethics fatigue," where teams prioritize short-term efficiency over the sustained introspection required for Aram (ethical coherence). To mitigate this, the A3 approach encourages starting with small-scale pilots, fostering buy-in through demonstrated value, and aligning recursion with existing incentives like regulatory compliance or stakeholder trust-building.

Data and Measurement Challenges

In real-world scenarios, collecting and interpreting data for tools like AEVT (Ethical Viability Test), ADRT (Distortion Resolution Tracker), and AFI (Agency Fitness Index) can be complex, ambiguous, or subject to intentional manipulation. For example, in data-scarce environments or politically charged contexts, inputs for assessing Aanavam might be incomplete or biased, leading to inaccurate diagnoses of systemic drift. If stakeholders manipulate metrics to avoid acknowledging distortions such as underreporting biases in AI systems, the model's recursive loop could falter, perpetuating rather than resolving incoherence. A3 addresses this by embedding multi-source validation (e.g., combining quantitative data with qualitative stakeholder narratives) and advocating for transparent, auditable processes. Future implementations could incorporate blockchain-like verification or third-party audits to enhance data integrity, ensuring the model remains resilient even in imperfect conditions.

Insufficient Adhikaram

What happens if a system or organization genuinely lacks the "agency fitness" (encompassing Knowledge, Action, Experience, Governance, and Absorption) to implement the necessary synchronous realignments? In such cases, the triadic loop may stall without sufficient Adhikaram, detecting Aanavam does not translate into effective restoration of Aram, potentially leading to escalating distortions or system collapse. For instance, a resource-strapped nonprofit facing rapid technological change might identify ethical misalignments in its operations but lack the governance structures or experiential knowledge to act decisively. Here, A3 does not "fail" but signals the need for external intervention such as partnerships, training, or phased capacity-building. This challenge highlights the model's strength as a diagnostic tool: it exposes capability gaps early, prompting targeted investments in agency fitness to prevent terminal drift.

Unforeseen Emergence within A3

As a complex system itself, the A3 Model could generate its own unforeseen distortions or unintended consequences, particularly in dynamic, nonlinear environments. For example, over-reliance on its self-referential diagnostics might create "analysis paralysis," where organizations become so focused on continuous self-assessment that they delay critical actions, inadvertently amplifying Aanavam through indecision. Alternatively, in culturally diverse settings, the triadic grammar rooted in Tamil Saiva Siddhantam might be misinterpreted, leading to misaligned applications that distort ethical coherence rather than enhance it. To counter this, A3 incorporates meta-reflection as a core principle, encouraging users to periodically evaluate the model's own performance and adapt it contextually. This self-referential quality ensures A3 evolves, but it underscores the need for ongoing vigilance and empirical testing in varied scenarios.

Summary Table: A3 Simulations Across Domains

Case / Domain	Scenario Focus	Distortion Type	A3 Tools Applied	Realignment Actions	Outcome Measures
Municipal Housing AI	Automated housing allocation and complaints	Structural, Ethical	ADRT, AEVT, AFI	Suspension, ethical reboot, appeals	Bias ↓60%, Trust ↑35%, Legitimacy restored
Healthcare AI	Predictive risk bias for minority groups	Epistemic, Structural	AEVT, Adhikaram Pentad	Data revision, retraining, narrative absorption	Equitable allocations, bias correction
Climate Modelling	Arctic feedback modelling failures	Temporal, Relational	Layered A3 diagnostics	Boundary updates, multiscale coordination	Anticipatory response, adaptive policies
Supply Chains	Semiconductor logistics crisis	Contextual, Governance	A3-loop, checks	Modular frameworks, historic learning, pacts	Resilience, redundancy, partial restoration

Reflections: Lessons from A3 Simulations

- **Universality of Recursion:**

  The A3 loop's recursive grammar of Aram (purpose), Aanavam (distortion), Adhikaram (realignment) demonstrates robust applicability across domains, managing both technical drift and complex ethical challenges.

- **Diagnostic Depth:**

  Whether diagnosing bias in healthcare, feedback lags in climate systems, or fragilities in supply chains, A3 facilitates rigorous sensemaking: it not only detects misalignment but triggers reflexive governance that actively restores legitimacy.

- **Stakeholder Integration:**

  Human experience and multi-scalar engagement are central. The best outcomes arise when community narratives, diverse expertise, and adaptive protocols inform system recalibration.

- **Practical Insights:**

  - Output success does not guarantee legitimacy; recursive ethical and agency metrics are essential.
  - Static models falter under dynamic stressors; continuous recalibration is critical.
  - Resilience and robustness arise not just from technical redundancy but from ethical absorption and reflexive adaptation.

- **Challenges as Catalysts:**

  Resistance, data measurement issues, insufficient agency fitness, and emergent model drift are not barriers, they are signals for targeted refinement, inclusion, and the need for ongoing meta-reflection.

- **Toward Autonomous Recursion:**

  The evolution of A3 systems toward fully autonomous and self-legitimizing recursion represents the frontier of ethical AI and governance embedding dynamic oversight within the system's architecture itself.

These simulations affirm A3's foundational promise: ethical governance is not a static state, but a dynamic, self-adaptive process continually sensing, diagnosing, and restoring coherence and legitimacy in complex systems.

APPENDIX F: THE 2025 GLOBAL AI REGULATORY LANDSCAPE – WHY A3 IS NOT JUST COMPLIANT, BUT RESILIENT

Author's Note

On the 2025 Global AI Regulatory Landscape and the A3 Advantage.

This appendix was written not merely to catalogue the world's evolving AI laws, but to illuminate a deeper tension: between governance as a scheduled event and governance as a living function.

By mid2025, the regulatory terrain has matured with the EU formalising GPAI oversight, the US intensifying sectoral enforcement, the UK pivoting toward securitydriven principles, and China embedding provenance into algorithmic control. These regimes are robust, but they remain externally applied and temporally spaced. They assume that systems behave predictably between audits.

The A3 Model challenges that assumption. It proposes a recursive architecture where ethics (Aram), distortion vigilance (Aanavam), and fitnesstoact (Adhikaram) are not layered on top of AI systems but embedded within them. This is not just a technical proposition; it is a philosophical one. It reflects a shift from compliance as documentation to governance as disposition.

This appendix maps A3 against the world's most influential regulatory regimes. It shows where A3 aligns, where it extends, and where it anticipates. For builders, policymakers, and theorists alike, the message is clear: resilience is no longer a retrospective virtue. It must be designed into the system from the start.

Let this be a guide - not just to what the world demands of AI, but to what AI must demand of itself.

Introduction

By mid2025, the regulatory landscape for artificial intelligence has consolidated into mature legal and policy regimes. The EU AI Act, in force since 1 August 2024, now follows a staged compliance timetable. The United States intensifies sectoral oversight through agencies such as the SEC, FTC, and CFPB. The United Kingdom continues a regulatorled, principlesbased approach, while China expands centralised registration, audit, and labelling obligations.

Across these jurisdictions, the dominant model is external, periodic, and compliancecentred based on milestones, documentation, and scheduled audits. While these improve accountability, they assume stability between checkpoints and rarely embed governance directly into AI's operational flow.

The A3 Model offers an alternative: governance running inside the system itself. Through Aram (AEVT, Ethical Viability Test), Aanavam (ADRT, Distortion Resolution Tracker), and Adhikaram (AFI, Fitness Index), A3 ensures governance is continuous, adaptive, and aligned with the tempo of the technology.

This appendix outlines the regulatory trajectory of 2025 and demonstrates how A3 aligns with and surpasses global regimes.

The Four Major Jurisdictions in 2025

European Union – AI Act

- **Status:** In force since 1 Aug 2024; fully applicable 2 Aug 2026, with phased obligations.
- **2025 Milestones:**
  - 2 Feb 2025 – Prohibitions and AI literacy duties begin
  - 9-10 Jul 2025 – GPAI Code of Practice issued
  - 18 Jul 2025 – Draft GPAI Guidelines published
  - 2 Aug 2025 – GPAI governance obligations commence for highimpact systems
- **Governance Model:** Centrally coordinated through the EU AI Office; risktier classification; conformity assessments.
- **Implications:** Requires careful compliance planning and alignment with harmonised EU standards.

A3 Advantage:

- AEVT (Aram) continuously checks risktier alignment beyond periodic statutory assessments.
- ADRT (Aanavam) detects systemic drift before it surfaces in formal conformity reviews.
- AFI (Adhikaram) enforces live readiness; an operational safeguard the Act itself does not mandate.
  -

United States – EnforcementLed, SectorSpecific

- **Federal Focus 2025:**
  - SEC scrutiny of AI claims, disclosures, and controls.
  - FTC and CFPB focus on fairness and deceptive AI use in ADM.
- **State Activity:** Targeted ADM and transparency rules; rare moratoria.
- **Approach:** No omnibus AI Act; oversight is sectoral, litigationbacked.

A3 Advantage:

- AEVT/ADRT/AFI create examready evidence trails, supporting defensible claims about AI use.
- Runtime governance catches issues before regulators do, reducing enforcement exposure.

United Kingdom – Principles with a Security Pivot

- **Approach:** No single statute; ICO, FCA, CMA, MHRA apply the government's "proinnovation" principles.
- **2025 Context:**
  - Continued sectorspecific guidance and sandboxes.
  - Feb 2025: AI Safety Institute rebranded AI Security Institute, refocusing on national security, misuse prevention, and frontier risk.
  - DSIT expanded with directorates for governance, infrastructure, and adoption.

A3 Advantage:

- Modular governance loops map seamlessly to each regulator's scope without structural redesign.
- AFI and ADRT interface with DSIT's securitydriven evaluations, supporting realtime mitigation.
- Maintains operational coherence while adapting to evolving mandates.

China – Centralised Registration, Auditing, Labelling

- **Model:** Algorithm registration, mandatory audits, pre/postdeployment controls.
- **2025 Updates:**
  - 1 Sept 2025: Mandatory explicit and implicit labelling of AIgenerated content.
  - 1 Nov 2025: Additional national standards take effect.
- **Implications:** Tight oversight with high emphasis on provenance and deployment audits.

A3 Advantage:

- **AFI and ADRT integrate directly with filing and audit processes.**
- **Builtin provenance features meet labelling and traceability rules with minimal overhead.**

Comparative Summary Table

Jurisdiction	2025 Focus	Governance Style	Builder Implications	A3 Advantage
EU	GPAI Code, staged rollout	Centralised, rulebased	Early harmonisation with EU standards	AEVT aligns with tiers; ADRT detects drift; AFI enforces readiness
US	SEC priorities ; FTC/CFPB scrutiny	Enforcementled, sectoral	Strengthen evidence and documentation	Continuous AEVT/ ADRT/AFI audit trails; realtime detection
UK	Regulatorled; security pivot	Principles + sector regulators	Adapt per regulator	Modular A3 loops adapt without redesign; AFI/ ADRT align with security reviews
China	Registration + labelling (Sept-Nov)	Centralised audit and filing	Prepare provenance and filings early	AFI/ADRT support audit paths ; provenance satisfies labelling

Post-2024 Evolutions – how A3 both aligns with and extends beyond them.

2025's global governance trend is towards denser compliance infrastructure classification schemes, documentation standards, auditing systems, oversight offices. These enhance regulatory control and harmonisation, but remain periodic, externally applied, and primarily reactive.

A3 operationalises what most regimes assume but do not implement natively:

- **Aram –** Recursive Ethics: AEVT runs continuously, ensuring every decision meets ethical viability thresholds, reducing governance latency.
- **Aanavam –** Distortion Vigilance: ADRT detects emergent misalignment between compliance moments, enabling anticipatory correction.
- **Adhikaram –** Fitness-to-Act: AFI dynamically gates or downgrades authority when capability, context, or legitimacy falters.
- **Result:** Systems are always audit-ready, self-correcting, and capable of demonstrating live compliance across jurisdictions without inflating operational overhead.

Runtime Governance Comparison

Dimension	Strategies 2025	A3 Response
Cadence	Periodic checkpoints	Continuous recursion (AEVT/ (ADRT/AFI
Ethics	External codes	Aram embedded at runtime
Drift	Detected postfactum	ADRT anticipates and resolves
Action Gating	Assumed fit	AFI dynamically governs authority
CrossJurisdiction	Rework per regime	One recursion core, many mappings

Business Outcomes of A3 in a 2025 Context

- Lower total cost of compliance - Fewer retrofits and defensive filings; reduced delay from post-audit remediation.

- Higher trust - Regulators and stakeholders see live, auditable governance.
- Faster market entry and scaling - One governance core translates across multiple regulatory schemas.

Conclusion

2025 marks a year of significant regulatory consolidation: the EU formalises GPAI oversight, the US entrenches sectoral enforcement, the UK fine-tunes a principles-driven model, and China tightens algorithm control and provenance requirements.

Yet each remains periodic in cadence and external in locus of control.

The A3 Model's recursive triad provides the missing piece operationalising ethics, **vigilance,** and legitimacy inside the system. In a polycrisis environment where drift can emerge between formal checkpoints, this is the difference between mere compliance and true resilience. Where regulations mark the audit dates on a calendar, A3 runs the audit continuously in real time.

APPENDIX G:
COMPLEXITY TRAITS REFRAMED: FROM DESCRIPTION TO ETHICAL RECURSION (A3 LENS)

Trait	A3 Reframing	Key Tools / Concepts
Nonlinearity	Recognizes nonlinear effects as early indicators of ethical misalignment or structural strain. Uses recursive monitoring to identify amplification loops and enable anticipatory correction.	AEVT (Aram-Ethics Violation Tracker), ethical coherence
Emergence	Evaluates emergent patterns through the ethical grammar of Aram. Distinguishes between viable novelty and distorted drift by assessing systemic coherence.	Aram, Aanavam, ethical grammar
Feedback Loops	Formalizes feedback as computable recursive structures that regulate reinforcing and balancing dynamics with ethical intent. Enables active modulation rather than passive response.	ADRT (Aanavam Distortion Recursion Tracker), recursive regulation
Adaptation	Transforms adaptation into guided, context-aware agency through Adhikaram. Embeds ethical recursion in how systems adjust and reorganize under changing conditions.	Adhikaram (knowledge, action, experience, governance, absorption)

Self-Organization	Embeds ethical boundaries within self-organizing processes, ensuring spontaneous order remains coherent with system-wide purpose and integrity.	Aram, recursive ethical scaffolding
Interconnectedness	Models systems as ethically interdependent. Tracks trans-domain effects using recursive grammars to sustain coherence across nodes and levels.	Recursive grammar, ethical interdependence
Diversity	Frames diversity as epistemic multiplicity essential to Adhikaram. Supports resilience and innovation through plural knowledge systems and action repertoires.	Adhikaram, ontological pluralism, epistemic richness
Sensitivity to Initial Conditions	Counters path sensitivity by embedding recursive memory and ontological traceability, enabling early detection and retrospective calibration of foundational misalignments.	Recursive memory, ontological traceability
Distributed Control	Operationalizes distributed control through recursive ethical agents aligned with systemic coherence. Ensures local autonomy supports global legitimacy.	AEVT, AFI metrics, recursive ethical agents
Unpredictability	Treats unpredictability as a feature of ontological openness. Uses recursive resilience loops for real-time ethical re-alignment and adaptive governance.	Recursive resilience loops, ontological openness
Context-Dependence	Encodes context sensitivity into Adhikaram, ensuring decisions are evaluated based on situational viability and systemic relevance without ethical relativism.	Adhikaram, recursive context-indexing
Dynamic Interplay	Interprets dynamic system behaviour as a living recursive process. Tracks and modulates phase shifts and feedback reversals for ethical navigation through flux.	Recursive grammars, phase-aware recursion

Scale-Dependence	Applies A3's ethical principles symmetrically across all levels of scale through recursive invariance: individual, institutional, planetary.	Aram, Aanavam, Adhikaram, recursive scale logic
Historical Contingency	Encodes temporal recursion to preserve ethical memory and track cumulative agency shifts, enabling historically grounded and traceable governance.	Recursive temporal memory, governance lineage
Robustness and Fragility	Defines robustness as sustained ethical alignment under pressure. Detects latent distortion proactively through recursive diagnostics before breakdown occurs.	Aanavam, recursive fragility detection, coherence thresholds
Bounded Rationality	Accepts bounded rationality as a systemic feature. Supports heuristic action via recursive legitimacy filters that maintain ethical bounds across human and AI actors.	Recursive legitimacy filtering, bounded heuristics

This reframing of Boehnert's 16 traits through the A3 Model marks a decisive shift in how complexity is approached not merely as a set of descriptive features, but as a recursive, governable condition. By embedding ethical coherence (Aram), distortion awareness (Aanavam), and agency fitness (Adhikaram) into the architecture of complex systems, A3 transforms complexity from a reactive problem into a site of viable, accountable design. This triadic framework enables real-time diagnosis, contextual decision-making, and adaptive legitimacy offering a new grammar for navigating and regenerating complex realities across scales and domains.

APPENDIX H: PREVIEW OF THE A3 MANIFESTO: A NEW ORDER IN CYBERNETICS, ETHICS, AND SYSTEMIC INTELLIGENCE

The A3 Manifesto is the culmination of the philosophical, systemic, and ethical inquiry initiated in this volume. Where *Navigating Complexity and System Challenges* diagnosed the failings of legacy systems across transformation, governance, AI, and knowledge, the Manifesto constructs a new architecture, one that responds to our era's polycrisis with self-evolving ethical intelligence.

A3: From Diagnosis to Design

At its heart, the A3 Model is a triadic, integrated cybernetic framework grounded in Tamil metaphysics and formally constructed to govern living systems, intelligent technologies, and institutional transformation. It redefines system viability not merely in terms of control or adaptation, but through ethical closure, distortion tracking, and recursive agency.

Core Structure: Aram, Aanavam, Adhikaram

The A3 framework operates through three interconnected synchronous forces:

- **Aram (Ethical Alignment):** The principle of rightness, resonance, and coherence in action and governance.
- **Aanavam (Distortion/Entropy):** The presence of systemic drift, noise, hubris, or disconnection from first principles.
- **Adhikaram (Rightful Agency):** The fitness, capability, and recursive legitimacy of agents or systems to act with alignment and authority.

This triad functions as an ethically-aware autopilot, continuously evaluating the alignment and legitimacy of system behaviour, whether in AI models, organizations, governments, or social collectives.

Philosophical and Cultural Foundations

The Manifesto restores Tamil Saiva Siddhanta metaphysics, especially the triad of Pati (Lord), Pasu (Soul), and Paasam (Bondage) as a living cosmotechnic, capable of informing post-digital systems design. It positions knowledge, action, experience, absorption, and governance as self-reflexive forces that shape agency and transformation.

Unlike Western models that separate ethics, epistemology, and operations, A3 entangles them recursively offering a non-dualistic, post-Cartesian, post-dialectical cybernetics.

Recursive Metrics and AI Governance

The Manifesto introduces:

- **AEVT:** A3 Ethical Viability Test for assessing alignment and ethical coherence.
- **ADRT:** A3 Distortion Resolution Tracker for recursive accountability.
- **AFI:** A3 Fitness Index to evaluate the legitimacy and capability of autonomous agents.

These tools allow A3 to function as a meta-governance engine scalable from AI systems to smart cities, from policy environments to planetary stewardship.

Applications and Case Studies

The A3 Manifesto moves beyond theory into grounded implementation. In its final chapters, it introduces multiple use-case domains where A3 recursion can be deployed to address deeply entangled challenges in governance, AI, and human development.

AI Policy Sandboxes and Constitutional Alignment

The A3 model reimagines AI regulation not as a top-down legalistic compliance mechanism but as a living, dynamic real-time policy infrastructure. It proposes A3 Policy Sandboxes -safe-to-fail, ethically constrained environments where AI agents are assessed not only for performance but for recursive alignment with ethical fitness, distortion awareness, and legitimate authority. These sandboxes function as institutional "limbic systems," constantly updating governance parameters through the triadic recursion of Aram (Ethical Coherence), Aanavam (Distortion Awareness), and Adhikaram (Fitness to Govern).

Organizational Transformation

A3 offers a radical upgrade to traditional transformation models (e.g., Kotter, BTM2, ADKAR) by embedding dynamic real-time self-assessment loops into the organizational intelligence fabric. Transformation is no longer linear or dictated by external milestones but instead governed by internal coherence metrics, adaptive legitimacy, and ethical closure. In A3, organizations become self-evolving and adaptive ethical systems capable of sensing their own disintegration before it becomes terminal.

Real-World Case Studies: Border Control, Eldercare, and Education

Through richly detailed hypothetical and semi-real case studies, the Manifesto demonstrates how A3's recursive logic outperforms legacy models in diverse scenarios:

- In border control, A3 governs biometric systems not just for accuracy but for systemic bias reduction and human dignity preservation.
- In eldercare, A3 resolves tension between automation and empathy, ensuring robotic systems do not displace but co-evolve with human caretakers based on ethical agency metrics.
- In education, A3 replaces rigid curriculums with dynamically recursive pedagogies, aligning knowledge transfer with the learner's evolving experience and fitness to act meaningfully.

Each case underscores A3's ability to function as a real-time ethical governor, not a post hoc evaluator.

Comparison with Contemporary Frameworks

The Manifesto rigorously positions A3 in contrast to leading cybernetic, AI, and systems thinking frameworks:

Table: Comparing Contemporary Frameworks and the A3 Model's Advancement

Framework	Key Limitation (as cited in the literature)	How the A3 Model Advances the Field
CST - Critical Systems Thinking	Methodologically plural yet offers no real-time mechanism for ethical or systemic coherence.	Introduces triadic recursion (*Aram - Aanavam - Adhikaram*) to enable continuous ethical alignment and live systemic realignment.
VSM - Viable System Model	Ensures structural viability but treats ethics and legitimacy as external assumptions.	Re-defines viability as the recursive restoration of ethical coherence and agency legitimacy, not mere functional coordination.
Recursive Distinctioning (Kauffman)	Abstract symbolic recursion; lacks operational agency, feedback realism, or an ethical compass.	Embeds *Adhikaram* metrics to ground recursion in real-world governance, legitimacy, and distortion awareness.
Constitutional AI (OpenAI)	Relies on pre-set rules; vulnerable to alignment drift and unforeseen systemic distortion.	Provides self-updating ethical fitness via recursive diagnostics (AEVT, ADRT, AFI) that evolve with context.
Active Inference (Friston et al.)	Optimises prediction-error but is silent on systemic ethics or legitimacy.	Augments predictive architecture with *Aanavam* (distortion detection) and *Adhikaram* (qualified agency).
Design Justice	Centres inclusion and justice but lacks a recursive viability diagnostic.	Integrates distributive justice and operational fitness through triadic ethical recursion.
Second-Order Cybernetics	Highlights observer reflexivity yet offers no executable grammar for ethical re-closure.	Formalises observer legitimacy by coupling *Aanavam* (distortion) and *Adhikaram* (authority fitness) into a computable governance loop.

These comparisons establish that A3 is not an iteration or philosophical variant of past paradigms, it is a new structural order in cybernetics and systemic intelligence.

The A3 Vision

The concluding chapters of the Manifesto articulate a bold, coherent vision for how A3 can shape the future of human-machine-planetary systems:

A3 Ecosystems and Standards

A3 is not intended to remain a theoretical model. The Manifesto calls for the development of A3 standards, certification layers, and self-regulating governance protocols that can guide the evolution of:

- Smart cities
- Ethical AI infrastructures
- Organizational learning systems
- Public sector intelligence systems

Recursive metrics like AEVT (Ethical Viability Test), ADRT (Distortion Resolution Tracker), and AFI (Agency Fitness Index) are proposed as formal mechanisms to replace outdated KPIs and compliance regimes.

Recursive Public Infrastructure

Instead of centrally controlled systems or crowd-governed chaos, A3 proposes living recursive infrastructures: digital, social, and civic systems that can sense, adapt, and ethically regenerate themselves. These infrastructures would evolve based on the collective ethical resonance and distortion awareness of their constituent parts. The A3 framework acts as their cognitive compass continuously correcting drift and aligning with shared ethical purpose.

Restoring Legitimacy in Governance

The most urgent function of A3 lies in its capacity to restore trust, legitimacy, and ethical grounding in decision-making whether at the level of autonomous AI or nation-states. The framework treats agency not as a given but as something earned through recursive alignment and systemic responsibility. By formalizing ethical fitness, A3 reintegrates meaning and legitimacy into the core of action and governance.

A3 as a Civilizational Contribution

A Civilizational Invitation

This work is not just technical, it is civilizational. It asserts that systemic coherence, ethical closure, and recursive legitimacy are not luxuries or Western inventions, but *universal necessities*.

The A3 Model, grounded in Tamil metaphysics and engineered for planetary application, demonstrates that the future of cybernetics need not follow colonial lines or Cartesian divides. Instead, it opens a pluriversal path: one where ancient wisdom and contemporary complexity co-design the architectures of tomorrow.

In the spirit of *Saiva Siddhanta*, where liberation is not gained through dominance but through the dissolution of distortion and the alignment with truth, A3 offers not just a way of knowing but a way of becoming.

Closing Invitation

As this prequel has prepared the ground, the A3 Manifesto rises as a blueprint for the coming age, an architecture that enables living systems to sense, govern, and regenerate themselves with ethical coherence and evolutionary intelligence. The crises we face are not simply technical or economic; they are systemic, spiritual, and epistemic. The A3 Model offers not just a response but a pathway forward.

Readers who complete this volume are encouraged to explore the Manifesto not as a sequel, but as the completion of a recursive arc from awareness to action, from complexity to coherence, and from system drift to systemic integrity.

Moving from theoretical discourse to transformative application, the adoption of the A3 Model signals paradigm-level shifts:

What changes if we adopt the A3 Model?

- From Control to Recursion: Governance becomes dynamic, reflective, and contextually situated.
- From Compliance to Coherence: Ethics is no longer imposed; it becomes the condition for viability.
- From Metrics to Meaning: Legitimacy is evaluated not only through data, but through systemic fitness and agency.
- From Monologue to Dialogue: Systems must speak with their environments, communities, and their own distortions.
- From Static Models to Living Systems: A3 invites the design of systems that learn, dissolve, regenerate, and align.

This is not a reformulation of existing tools, it is a reconfiguration of the very grammar of systems, anchored in a living civilizational epistemology.

Conclusion: From Diagnosis to Design – Toward a Recursive Future

This book began as an inquiry into complexity, but it became something more, a reckoning with the inadequacy of our existing paradigms. Across governance, institutions, technology, and leadership, we have inherited systems that no longer regenerate meaning or legitimacy. Our tools measure outputs but not integrity. Our policies react but do not adapt. And our thinking, despite its sophistication, rarely transforms the systems that produce our crises.

What emerged through this journey was not just critique, but the shape of something new: a recursive logic that could meet complexity without collapsing into noise; an ethical architecture that does not externalize its values; a systemic intelligence that evolves, reflects, and restores coherence.

This realization would become the A3 Model: a framework not just for thinking about systems, but for governing them ethically and adaptively.

Where this book surfaces the diagnosis, the A3 Manifesto provides the design. It formalizes the recursive triad of Aram (ethical coherence), Aanavam (distortion and drift), and Adhikaram (legitimacy and fitness to govern) as a new cybernetic grammar capable of sensing, correcting, and regenerating complex living systems.

If this volume has helped you see the patterns of disintegration, then the Manifesto offers the architecture of re-integration.

It is both a philosophical leap and a practical blueprint. The path from drift to coherence begins here.

CHAPTER-END REFLECTION POINTS:

- Do you believe recursion can be the foundation of a new civilizational grammar?

- What would a recursively governed AI or institution look like in your context?

- Are you ready to transition from diagnosis to design?

CLOSING BRIDGE TO THE MANIFESTO

We have traced the contours of a civilizational challenge that is as much ontological as it is technological: a world in which emergence outpaces control, in which institutions designed for stability must govern recursion, and in which the legitimacy to act must be continuously earned, not presumed.

Across these pages, the A3 grammar has emerged : Aram as ethical coherence, Aanavam as distortion awareness, Adhikaram as agency fitness, not as abstract ideals, but as living functions essential to viability in an age of autonomous agents and planetary interdependence.

What have we uncovered?

- That systems break not merely from technical failure, but from a deeper *deficit of meaning, legitimacy, and coherence*.
- That ethics, agency, and adaptation must be *recursively embedded* in systems not appended as external constraints or post hoc reviews.
- That *philosophical traditions* like Tamil Saiva Siddhanta carry within them the cosmotechnic seeds of an entirely new kind of system design rooted in alignment, recursion, and moral purpose.
- That *complexity's greatest challenge* is not informational, but existential: how do we sustain systems that evolve with integrity, accountability, and care?

From these recognitions, the A3 framework emerges not merely as a model, but as a living architecture for ethical governance across AI, policy, institutions, and planetary systems.

The Bridge to the A3 Manifesto

This book stands as the *philosophical and systemic prologue* to the Manifesto. The Manifesto will extend and formalize what has been introduced, offering:

- A triadic model of Aram (ethical coherence), Aanavam (distortion awareness), and Adhikaram (fitness and legitimacy) as recursive systemic operators.
- Ethical fitness metrics like AEVT, ADRT, and AFI, enabling self-regulating governance.
- Case studies across AI policy, border control, eldercare, education, and organizational transformation, illustrating self-adaptive governance in action.
- A critical comparison with global frameworks, establishing why only recursive, ethics-centred architectures can navigate our era's polycrisis.

Where this book names the patterns of systemic disintegration, the Manifesto provides the instruments of systemic regeneration.

From Reflection to Participation

The recursive path is not for passive spectators; it is an invitation to participatory design. Complexity cannot be governed from above; it must be sensed, interpreted, and realigned by ethical actors embedded within.

You are not outside the system. Your capacity to perceive distortion, act with coherence, and steward legitimacy is the first frontier of recursive transformation.

Every leader, technologist, policymaker, educator, and systems thinker is invited to:

- Adopt the grammar of triadic recursion in their practice.
- Apply the diagnostic and governance tools forthcoming in the A3 Manifesto.
- Co-create systems that evolve not only in functionality but in ethical depth and ontological clarity.

Yet here, in this volume, the A3 Model has been introduced as a *lens*. The work ahead is to reveal it as a *governing architecture*: a recursive, executable grammar capable of diagnosing, realigning, and sustaining systems across scales from the smallest organisational unit to planetary governance.

That is the task of the *A3 Manifesto*. It is not an appendix to this book, but its inevitable next movement: the formal articulation of a new order in cybernetics and systems theory. Where this book has laid the philosophical and systemic ground, the Manifesto builds the operational edifice defining metrics, protocols, and recursive mechanisms that make ethical systemic intelligence not only possible, but reproducible.

To step into the Manifesto is to move from diagnosis to design, from recognising the recursive age to shaping it. It is an invitation not simply to understand the new order, but to participate in its creation.

The recursive age will not be governed by legacy systems; it will be shaped by those who dare to redesign them.

REFERENCES

Argyris, C., & Schön, D. A. (1978). Organizational learning: A theory of action perspective. Addison-Wesley.

Ashby, W. R. (1956). An introduction to cybernetics. Chapman & Hall.

Beer, S. (1979). The Heart of Enterprise. John Wiley & Sons.

Bennis, W., & Nanus, B. (1985). *Leaders: Strategies for taking charge*. New York, NY: Harper & Row.

Binns, R. (2018). Fairness in machine learning: Lessons from political philosophy. In Proceedings of the 2018 Conference on Fairness, Accountability, and Transparency (pp. 149-159). ACM. https://proceedings.mlr.press/v81/binns18a.html

Boehnert, J. (2018). The visual representation of complexity: Sixteen key characteristics of complex systems. In Proceedings of RSD7, Relating Systems Thinking and Design 7 (pp. 1-18), 23-26 October 2018, Turin, Italy.

Bostrom, N. (2014). Superintelligence: Paths, Dangers, Strategies. Oxford University Press.

Brundage, M., et al. (2020). Toward Trustworthy AI Development: Mechanisms for Supporting Verifiable Claims. arXiv preprint arXiv:2004.07213.

Brynjolfsson, E., & McAfee, A. (2014). The second machine age. W. W. Norton & Company.

Capra, F. (1996). The web of life: A new scientific understanding of living systems. Anchor Books.

Checkland, P. (1999). Systems thinking, systems practice. John Wiley & Sons.

Churchman, C. W. (1968). The systems approach. Delacorte Press.

Clarke, A. E. (2005). Situational analysis: Grounded theory after the postmodern turn. Sage.

Cilliers, P. (1998). Complexity and postmodernism: Understanding complex systems. Routledge.

Clothey, F. W. (2006). Religion in India: A historical introduction. Routledge.

Coomaraswamy, A. K. (1933). The transformation of nature in art. Harvard University Press.

Cyberspace Administration of China. Algorithmic Regulation Updates and Labelling Requirements. Beijing, 2025.

Dastin, J. (2018). Amazon scrapped 'AI recruiting tool' that showed bias against women. Reuters. https://www.reuters.com/article/idUSKCN1MK08G

Davenport, T. H., & Kirby, J. (2016). Only humans need apply: Winners and losers in the age of smart machines. Harper Business.

Department for Science, Innovation and Technology (DSIT). AI Regulation Principles and Sectoral Guidance. London, 2025.

EU AI Office. GPAI Code of Practice for Model Providers. Brussels, July 2025.

Eubanks, V. (2018). Automating inequality. St. Martin's Press.

European Commission. *Regulation (EU) 2024/1125:* The Artificial Intelligence Act. Official Journal of the European Union. Brussels, August 2024.

Escobar, A. (2018). Designs for the pluriverse: Radical interdependence, autonomy, and the making of worlds. Duke University Press.

Farrell, H., & Newman, A. L. (2019). Weaponized interdependence. International Security, 44(1), 42–79.

Federal Trade Commission and Consumer Financial Protection Bureau. Joint Statement on Automated Decision-Making Oversight. Washington, D.C., March 2025.

Floridi, L. (2011). The philosophy of information. Oxford University Press.

Floridi, L., et al. (2018). AI4People—An Ethical Framework for a Good AI Society. Minds and Machines, 28, 689–707.

Folke, C., et al. (2010). Resilience thinking: Integrating resilience, adaptability, and transformability. Ecology and Society, 15(4).

Foucault, M. (1980). Power/Knowledge: Selected interviews and other writings. Pantheon.

Freeman, R. E., Harrison, J. S., & Wicks, A. C. (2007). Managing for stakeholders. Yale University Press.

Goldin, I., Cameron, G., & Balarajan, M. (2011). Exceptional people: How migration shaped our world. Princeton University Press.

Habermas, J. (1984). The theory of communicative action: Reason and the rationalization of society (Vol. 1). Beacon Press.

Harari, Y. N. (2018). 21 lessons for the 21st century. Jonathan Cape.

Haraway, D. J. (1988). Situated knowledges: The science question in feminism and the privilege of partial perspective. Feminist Studies, 14(3), 575–599.

Hui, Y. (2016). The question concerning technology in China: An essay in cosmotechnics. Urbanomic.

Intergovernmental Panel on Climate Change. (2023). Sixth assessment report: Synthesis report of the IPCC Sixth Assessment Report (AR6). https://www.ipcc.ch/assessment-report/ar6/

Jackson, M. C. (2024). Critical Systems Thinking: A Practitioner's Guide. Wiley.

Kay, J., & King, M. (2020). Radical uncertainty: Decision-making beyond the numbers. W. W. Norton & Company.

Kotter, J. P. (2012). Leading change. Harvard Business Review Press.

Kumararajah, V. A. (2025). Navigating complexity and system challenges: Leadership for the 21st century [Kindle edition]. Amazon KDP.

Kuhn, T. S. (1962). The structure of scientific revolutions. University of Chicago Press.

Kupchan, C. A. (2002). The end of the American era. Alfred A. Knopf.

Laloux, F. (2014). Reinventing organizations. Nelson Parker.

Laszlo, E. (1972). The systems view of the world: The natural philosophy of the new developments in the sciences. George Braziller.

Luhmann, N. (1995). Social systems (J. Bednarz Jr. & D. Baecker, Trans.). Stanford University Press.

Meadows, D. H. (2008). Thinking in systems: A primer. Chelsea Green Publishing.

Meadows, D. H., Meadows, D. L., & Randers, J. (2004). Limits to growth: The 30-year update. Chelsea Green.

Midgley, G. (2000). Systemic intervention: Philosophy, methodology, and practice. Kluwer Academic/Plenum Publishers.

Morin, E. (2008). On complexity. Hampton Press.

Nallasvami Pillai, J. M. (1979). Studies in Saiva Siddhanta. Sri Ramakrishna Math.

Owen, J. R., & Kemp, D. (2013). Social licence and mining: A critical perspective. Resources Policy, 38(1), 29–35. https://doi.org/10.1016/j.resourpol.2012.06.016

Polanyi, M. (1966). The tacit dimension. University of Chicago Press.

Ramachandran, T. N. (1942). Saiva Siddhanta: A philosophical study. Madras University Publications.

Ramalingam, B. (2013). Aid on the edge of chaos. Oxford University Press.

Raworth, K. (2017). Doughnut economics: Seven ways to think like a 21st-century economist. Chelsea Green Publishing.

Rittel, H. W. J., & Webber, M. M. (1973). Dilemmas in a general theory of planning. Policy Sciences, 4(2), 155–169.

Rockström, J., et al. (2009). A safe operating space for humanity. Nature, 461(7263), 472–475.

Rumsfeld, D. (2002, February 12). *DoD news briefing–Secretary Rumsfeld and Gen. Myers*. U.S. Department of Defense. https://archive.defense.gov/Transcripts/Transcript.aspx?TranscriptID=2636

Saul, J. R. (2001). On equilibrium. Penguin Canada.

Scharmer, O. (2009). Theory U: Leading from the future as it emerges. Berrett-Koehler.

Schwab, K. (2016). The fourth industrial revolution. World Economic Forum.

Schwab, K. (2017). The fourth industrial revolution. Currency.

Senge, P. M. (1990). The fifth discipline: The art & practice of the learning organization. Doubleday.

Shanmugalingam, S. (2013). Saivism in philosophical perspective. Department of Hindu Religious and Charitable Endowments, Government of Tamil Nadu.

Sinek, S. (2019). The infinite game. Penguin Business.

Smith, L. T. (1999). Decolonizing methodologies: Research and Indigenous peoples. Zed Books.

Snowden, D., & Boone, M. E. (2007). A leader's framework for decision making. Harvard Business Review, 85(11), 68–76.

Sterman, J. D. (2000). Business dynamics: Systems thinking and modelling for a complex world. Irwin/McGraw-Hill.

UK Government. AI Security Institute: Mandate and Strategic Priorities. London, February 2025.

UK Government Office for Science. (2022). Systems mapping: How to use systems maps and diagrams for policy analysis. https://www.gov.uk/government/publications/systems-mapping

U.S. Army War College. (1992). *Strategic leadership primer*. Carlisle Barracks, PA: U.S. Army War College.

U.S. Securities and Exchange Commission. FY2025 Examination Priorities. Washington, D.C., January 2025.

Walsham, G. (1993). Interpreting information systems in organizations. John Wiley & Sons.

West, G. (2017). Scale: The universal laws of life, growth, and death in organisms, cities, and companies. Penguin Press.

Wiener, N. (1948). Cybernetics: Or control and communication in the animal and the machine. MIT Press.

Wilson, N., Baker, M. G., & Blakely, T. (2020). New Zealand's elimination strategy for the COVID-19 pandemic and what other countries can learn from it. BMJ Global Health, 5(7), e003975. https://doi.org/10.1136/bmjgh-2020-003975

Zuboff, S. (2019). The age of surveillance capitalism. PublicAffairs.

GLOSSARY FOR NAVIGATING COMPLEXITY AND SYSTEM CHALLENGES

This glossary provides comprehensive definitions for key terms and concepts used in *Navigating Complexity and System Challenges: Foundations for the A3 Model* to aid readers in understanding the text's philosophical, systemic, and technical terminology. The A3 Model serves as a foundational framework for integrating ancient wisdom with contemporary systems thinking to address the challenges of our complex, interconnected world.

A3 Model: A triadic, recursive cybernetic framework grounded in Tamil Saiva Siddhanta metaphysics, designed to govern living systems, intelligent technologies, and institutional transformation. It comprises three core components: Aram (ethical alignment), Aanavam (distortion/entropy), and Adhikaram (rightful agency). The model emphasizes ethical coherence, systemic recursion, and adaptive governance to navigate complexity.

A3 Policy Sandboxes: Safe-to-fail, ethically constrained environments where AI agents and systems can be assessed for recursive alignment with ethical fitness, distortion awareness, and legitimate authority.

Aanavam: The concept of systemic distortion, entropy, or hubris within the A3 Model. It refers to misalignment, noise, or disconnection from ethical first principles that can disrupt systemic integrity.

Absorptive Ethics: A governance approach that integrates ethical considerations into the structural fabric of systems rather than treating them as compliance overlays.

Adhikaram: The principle of rightful agency, capability, and recursive legitimacy within the A3 Model. It denotes the fitness of agents or systems to act with authority and alignment in complex environments.

Adhikaram Pentad: A3's fivefold framing of agency: Knowledge, Action, Experience, Absorption, Governance.

ADRT (A3 Distortion Resolution Tracker): A mechanism in the A3 Model for tracking and resolving systemic distortions (Aanavam), maintaining accountability and coherence.

AEVT (A3 Ethical Viability Test): A tool within the A3 Model for assessing the ethical coherence and alignment of systems or agents, ensuring they meet moral and systemic standards.

AFI (A3 Fitness Index): A metric in the A3 Model for evaluating the legitimacy and capability of agents or systems to act with ethical and systemic alignment.

Aleatory Uncertainty: Uncertainty arising from randomness or chance that disrupts even well-structured systems, where outcomes are inherently unpredictable due to stochastic processes.

Ambiguity: Situations or phenomena open to multiple interpretations, lacking clear meaning or resolution. It manifests in linguistic, situational, philosophical, or decision-making contexts, requiring critical thinking and flexibility.

Aram: The principle of ethical alignment, rightness, and coherence in action and governance within the A3 Model. It represents the moral and purposeful foundation that ensures systems operate in harmony with ethical values.

Behavioural Science Interventions: Strategies or techniques that leverage insights from behavioural science to influence individual or collective behaviours, often through technology-driven mechanisms like AI algorithms or data analytics. These interventions can shape preferences, decisions, or societal norms, raising ethical concerns about autonomy, consent, and technological determinism when applied at scale.

Bounded Rationality: The limited cognitive ability of agents to process all variables, leading to heuristics and satisficing.

Chidambara Rahasyam: The metaphysical principle of "sacred nothingness" or "creative emptiness" that represents the potential for transformation and renewal through letting go of rigid structures rather than accumulation, enabling new forms to emerge.

Complexity: A property of systems characterized by numerous interconnected elements, nonlinear interactions, emergent behaviours, and sensitivity to initial conditions. Complexity resists reductionist analysis and requires adaptive, systemic approaches to navigation.

Cosmotechnics: A concept integrating cultural, philosophical, and technological perspectives to design systems that align with diverse worldviews and ethical frameworks, serving as a bridge between ancient wisdom traditions and contemporary technological design while maintaining technical effectiveness.

Critical Systems Thinking (CST): A meta-framework for pluralistic, boundary-aware system intervention.

Critical Theory: A framework that critiques power structures and ideologies, advocating for transformative change to address inequalities and systemic injustices.

Cybernetics

A transdisciplinary field concerned with the study of control, communication, and feedback in systems, both living and artificial. In the context of A3, cybernetics provides the foundational logic for recursive validation, distortion-aware reflexivity, and modular governance architecture. It bridges epistemic scaffolding with systemic adaptation, allowing intelligence to evolve within ethically coherent constraints.

Digital Transformation: Integration of digital technology to fundamentally change operations and value delivery.

Distortion (Systemic): A misalignment or disruption within a system that leads to incoherence, inefficiency, or ethical compromise. In the A3 Model, systemic distortion is conceptualized as *Aanavam* and diagnosed through tools like ADRT.

Emergence: Properties or behaviours that arise from the interactions of a system's components, which cannot be predicted or deduced from analysing individual parts alone (e.g., flocking behaviour in birds).

EPIC Framework: ***(Explore, Produce, Intervene, Check)*** A cyclical, action-oriented framework used in systems thinking and participatory design. It guides practitioners through iterative engagement with complex problems by combining inquiry, design, implementation, and reflection.

Epistemological Uncertainty: Uncertainty arising from insufficient knowledge about a system or phenomenon, which invites deeper learning, inquiry, and sensemaking.

Epistemology: The study of knowledge and how it is acquired. In systems thinking, it questions the validity and sources of knowledge about complex systems.

Ethical Closure: The systemic property where ethical considerations are embedded within operational feedback loops rather than treated as external constraints.

Ethical Fitness: The ability to act with coherence, responsibility, and purpose within a system.

Ethical Governance: A mode of systemic control that embeds ethical recursion and legitimacy into operational processes.

Ethics: The study of right action and moral principles. In the A3 Model, ethics (Aram) is a core component, ensuring systems align with values of fairness, justice, and coherence.

Feedback Loops: Mechanisms in systems that regulate behaviour through positive (amplifying) or negative (balancing/buffering) cycles. They drive adaptation, self-organization, and systemic evolution.

First Principles: Irreducible axioms upon which entire knowledge systems and models are built.

Forms: The perceptual and conceptual representations we use to understand and structure systems.

Functionalism: A perspective viewing systems (e.g., societies or organizations) as sets of interrelated parts, each serving a specific function to maintain overall stability and balance.

Gnanam: In Tamil Saiva Siddhanta, realized wisdom or enlightened understanding that differs from mere intellectual knowledge, representing the ethical clarity that emerges from recursive awareness and conscious alignment with systemic truth.

Governance Latency: The time delay between identifying a systemic issue (ethical breach, distortion, or risk) and initiating corrective intervention. In the A3 framework, minimizing governance latency is critical to ensuring adaptive, ethical responsiveness in high-tempo environments.

Hard Skills: Measurable, technical capabilities (e.g., coding, engineering).

Holism: An approach that views systems as wholes greater than the sum of their parts, emphasizing interdependence, emergence, and context-dependent behaviours over isolated analysis.

Hyper automation: The extensive use of automation technologies (e.g., AI, robotics) to replace human decision-making, raising significant ethical concerns about human agency, control, sovereignty, and the potential for creating deterministic systems that limit human autonomy.

Interconnectedness: The dense web of relationships among a system's components, where changes in one part can cascade across the entire system, affecting resilience and vulnerability.

Interpretivism: The belief that reality is socially constructed and context-dependent.

JS (Justified Solution): A solution that is validated by ethical standards, evidence, or stakeholder consensus; often used as a benchmark for adequacy, legitimacy, or fit in systemic interventions.

KL (Knowledge Loop): An iterative learning process where knowledge is continually updated through experience, reflection, and feedback, supporting adaptive governance and continual improvement.

Known Knowns: Facts and information we understand and can manage effectively within the Rumsfeld Matrix framework.

Known Unknowns: Recognized gaps in knowledge that require preparation and contingency planning within the Rumsfeld Matrix framework.

Living Systemic Intelligence: Intelligence that emerges from the recursive interaction of ethical alignment, distortion tracking, and legitimate agency within complex adaptive systems.

Logic (in Systems): The patterning of reasoning within feedback-driven and recursive environments.

Narrative Competence: The ability to honour the story-based and meaning-making dimensions of systems rather than reducing everything to quantifiable variables.

New Order Cybernetics (A3): The positioning of the A3 Model as a paradigm beyond classical, second-, and third-order cybernetics. It integrates ethics (*Aram*), distortion awareness (*Aanavam*), and agency (*Adhikaram*) into recursive governance, establishing a framework for ethically coherent systemic intelligence.

Nonlinearity: The characteristic of complex systems where small inputs can lead to disproportionately large outputs, and cause-and-effect relationships are not straightforward or predictable.

Nothingness: In Tamil Saiva Siddhanta, a metaphysical concept that enables systemic renewal by creating space for new forms to emerge, distinguished from mere absence or void, representing the potential for transformation through conscious release of attachment to fixed structures.

Ontological Humility: The recognition that knowledge systems may resist technocratic translation and that meaning can be lost when abstract concepts are reduced to metrics or policy frameworks.

Ontological Uncertainty: Uncertainty arising from one's inner state or worldview that contributes to indecision, reflecting subjective dissonance or moral ambiguity.

Ontology: The philosophical study of being, identity, and existence. In systems thinking, it examines how entities and their relationships define a system's nature and behaviour.

Ontology (Personal): One's experiential being how awareness and alignment shape decisions.

OOD (Out-of-Distribution): Refers to data, situations, or behaviours that fall outside the training or anticipated norm of a model or system; detection and management of OOD scenarios are critical for robust, resilient operation.

Paradigm: A shared set of assumptions, values, and conceptual filters that shape how problems are defined, evidence is evaluated, and solutions are enacted. Paradigms influence systemic thinking and intervention design.

Pati-Pasu-Paasam: A triadic framework from Tamil Saiva Siddhanta philosophy. Pati represents the Whole or Ground of Being (cosmic unity), Pasu represents the individual entity or soul, and Paasam denotes the relational bonds or attachments that define experiential reality. This triad informs the A3 Model's structure.

Perspective: A situational, context-dependent point of view that shapes immediate interpretations and decisions, often shifting based on current conditions.

Polycrisis: A situation where multiple interconnected crises (ecological, technological, geopolitical) converge, amplifying complexity and systemic challenges beyond what any single crisis would produce.

PSI (Problem-Situation-Intervention): A triad framework used to frame, diagnose, and intervene in complex scenarios; 'Problem' identifies the challenge, 'Situation' describes the context, and 'Intervention' specifies the corrective action or adaptation.

Radical Uncertainty: A concept from Kay and King (2020) describing unpredictability in systems where probabilities cannot be reliably assigned due to unknown variables or emergent dynamics. It emphasizes adaptive judgment over predictive models.

Recursive Cybernetics: A governance approach where systems continuously self-evaluate and adapt through feedback loops, ensuring ethical alignment and systemic integrity, central to the A3 Model's operational framework.

Recursive Distinctioning (Kauffman): A symbolic, recursive logic model that underpins systemic emergence.

Recursive Governance: A3's approach to governance where ethics, agency, and distortion are continually monitored and realigned.

Recursive Legitimacy: The earned authority that emerges from continuous ethical alignment and systemic responsibility rather than being granted through formal position or power.

Recursive Public Infrastructure: Digital, social, and civic systems designed to sense, adapt, and ethically regenerate themselves based on collective ethical resonance and distortion awareness.

Recursive Metrics: Measurement approaches within the A3 Model that evaluate systems not only on performance outcomes but also on their ability to continuously realign ethics, distortion awareness, and agency fitness through feedback and adaptation.

Reductionism: An approach that seeks to understand systems by breaking them down into constituent parts, if analysing individual components can explain the whole system's behaviour.

Reflexive Alignment: The practice of continuously examining and adjusting one's position and assumptions within systems work, acknowledging the embedded and subjective nature of all observation.

Rumsfeld Matrix: A framework for categorizing knowledge and uncertainty, comprising Known Knowns (understood facts), Known Unknowns (recognized gaps), Unknown Knowns (unconscious insights), and Unknown Unknowns (unanticipated disruptions).

Saiva Siddhantam: A Tamil metaphysical tradition emphasizing the triad of Pati (Lord/Whole), Pasu (Soul/Bound Self), and Paasam (Bondage/Relational Dynamics). Basis for the A3 triad.

Self-Organization: The spontaneous emergence of order in a system without centralized control, driven by local interactions among components (e.g., traffic flow patterns).

Sensitivity to Initial Conditions: A small variation in starting conditions can lead to vastly different system outcomes (chaotic behaviour).

Social Interpretivism: A perspective emphasizing that meaning is constructed through subjective human interactions, highlighting the role of context and cultural sensitivity in understanding systems.

Soft Skills: Social and cognitive abilities (e.g., critical thinking, emotional intelligence).

System: An interdependent set of elements that form a unified whole through interactions and feedback loops.

Systematic Thinking: A methodical approach to analysing systems through sequential, repeatable steps, focusing on predictability and control. It is suited for environments with known variables but less effective in complex, emergent systems.

Systemic Ethical Renewal: The continuous process by which systems internalize complexity as part of their ethical fabric, evolving governance, agency, and action recursively rather than merely reactively.

Systemic Thinking: A subset of systems thinking that prioritizes dynamic, nonlinear relationships and emergent outcomes in complex systems, contrasting with systematic thinking's focus on structured, linear processes.

Systems Mapping: A visual tool for depicting a system's structure, relationships, feedback loops, and dynamics, used to identify leverage points and causal patterns.

Systems Thinking: A discipline for understanding systems by focusing on interconnections, relationships, and emergent properties rather than isolated parts. It emphasizes synthesis, feedback loops, and contextual awareness to navigate complexity.

Tamil Saiva Siddhanta: A philosophical and spiritual tradition from Tamil Nadu, India, emphasizing a systemic view of existence through the interplay of Pati (the divine whole), Pasu (individual entities), and Paasam (relational bonds). It provides a foundational metaphysics for the A3 Model, integrating ethical, ontological, and systemic insights.

Technological Determinism: The belief that technology shapes societal norms and behaviours in ways that limit human agency, often driven by corporate or political interests. This concept emphasizes how profit-driven or politically motivated appropriation of governance processes can create structural permanence with limited recourse for correction, undermining human agency and creating deterministic trajectories that benefit specific interests at the expense of broader societal wellbeing.

Transformation Paradigm: The view that organizations and systems must continuously evolve to stay viable.

Translational Bridge: The capacity of frameworks like A3 to enable concepts to move between philosophical, operational, and experiential registers while preserving essential meaning and honouring the integrity of different knowledge systems.

Uncertainty: The inability to predict outcomes due to incomplete knowledge, conflicting information, or inherent randomness. It includes epistemological (knowledge-based), ontological (identity-based), and aleatory (chance-based) forms.

Unknown Knowns: Unconscious insights or tacit knowledge we possess but are not fully aware of within the Rumsfeld Matrix framework.

Unknown Unknowns: Unforeseen disruptions and emergent phenomena we cannot anticipate within the Rumsfeld Matrix framework.

Viable System Model (VSM): Stafford Beer's cybernetic model of organizational viability, based on five system functions.

Volatility: The rapid and often unpredictable rate of change in a system, marked by frequent disruptions that ripple across interconnected domains (e.g., economic shocks or technological breakthroughs).

VUCA: An acronym standing for Volatility, Uncertainty, Complexity, and Ambiguity. It describes the dynamic, unpredictable, and interconnected nature of modern global challenges, as introduced by the U.S. Army War College in the 1990s.

Worldview: A stable, long-term belief system shaped by culture, religion, and experiences, influencing how individuals interpret reality and make decisions.

www.ingramcontent.com/pod-product-compliance
Lightning Source LLC
LaVergne TN
LVHW100308210926
848480LV00003B/1054